IMPOSSIBLE THINGS

UNBELIEVABLE ANSWERS TO THE WORLD'S WEIRDEST QUESTIONS

IMPOSSIBLE THINGS

UNBELIEVABLE ANSWERS TO THE WORLD'S WEIRDEST QUESTIONS

wren
&rook

FROM PROFESSIONAL FACT HUNTER AND PODCAST SENSATION
DAN SCHREIBER
ILLUSTRATED BY KRISTYNA BACZYNSKI

First published in Great Britain in 2024 by Wren & Rook

Text copyright © Dan Schreiber 2024
Illustrations copyright © Kristyna Baczynski 2024
All rights reserved.

The right of Dan Schreiber and Kristyna Baczynski to be identified as the author and illustrator respectively of this Work has been asserted by them in accordance with the Copyright, Designs & Patents Act 1988.

ISBN: 978 1 5263 6638 2

Wren & Rook
An imprint of
Hachette Children's Group
Part of Hodder & Stoughton
Carmelite House
50 Victoria Embankment
London EC4Y 0DZ

An Hachette UK Company
www.hachette.co.uk
www.hachettechildrens.co.uk

Printed and bound in Great Britain by Clays Ltd, Elcograf S.p.A.

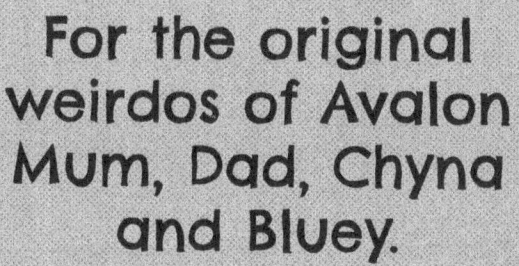

For the original weirdos of Avalon Mum, Dad, Chyna and Bluey.

And the new weirdos of Margate Fenella, Wilf, Ted and Kit.

CONTENTS

INTRODUCTION: 11
THE OD_D_YSSEY

CHAPTER 1: 21
WHERE IS THE BEST PLACE
TO NOT SEE A MONSTER?

CHAPTER 2: 43
DO GHOSTS EVER GET
BORED OF HAUNTING US?

CHAPTER 3: 69
ARE ROCK STARS
SECRETLY ALIENS?

CHAPTER 4: 89
ARE TIME TRAVELLERS
BAD PARTY GUESTS?

CHAPTER 5: 111
DO I NEED GLASSES FOR THE EYES
IN THE BACK OF MY HEAD?

CHAPTER 6: 135
SHOULD WE BE LEARNING TO SPEAK CAT?

CHAPTER 7: 151
CAN IMAGINARY FRIENDS
COME TO LIFE?

CHAPTER 8: 173
IS IT RUDE TO GIFT
SOMEONE A CURSED ITEM?

CHAPTER 9: 193
DID DINOSAURS BEAT US
TO THE MOON?

CHAPTER 10: 215
ARE WE ALL ACTUALLY LIVING IN A
GIANT VIDEO GAME SIMULATION?

EPILOGUE: 239
WHAT HAVE ZOMBIES EVER
DONE FOR US?

WARNING:

If you read a book about Impossible Things, Impossible Things start to happen to you.

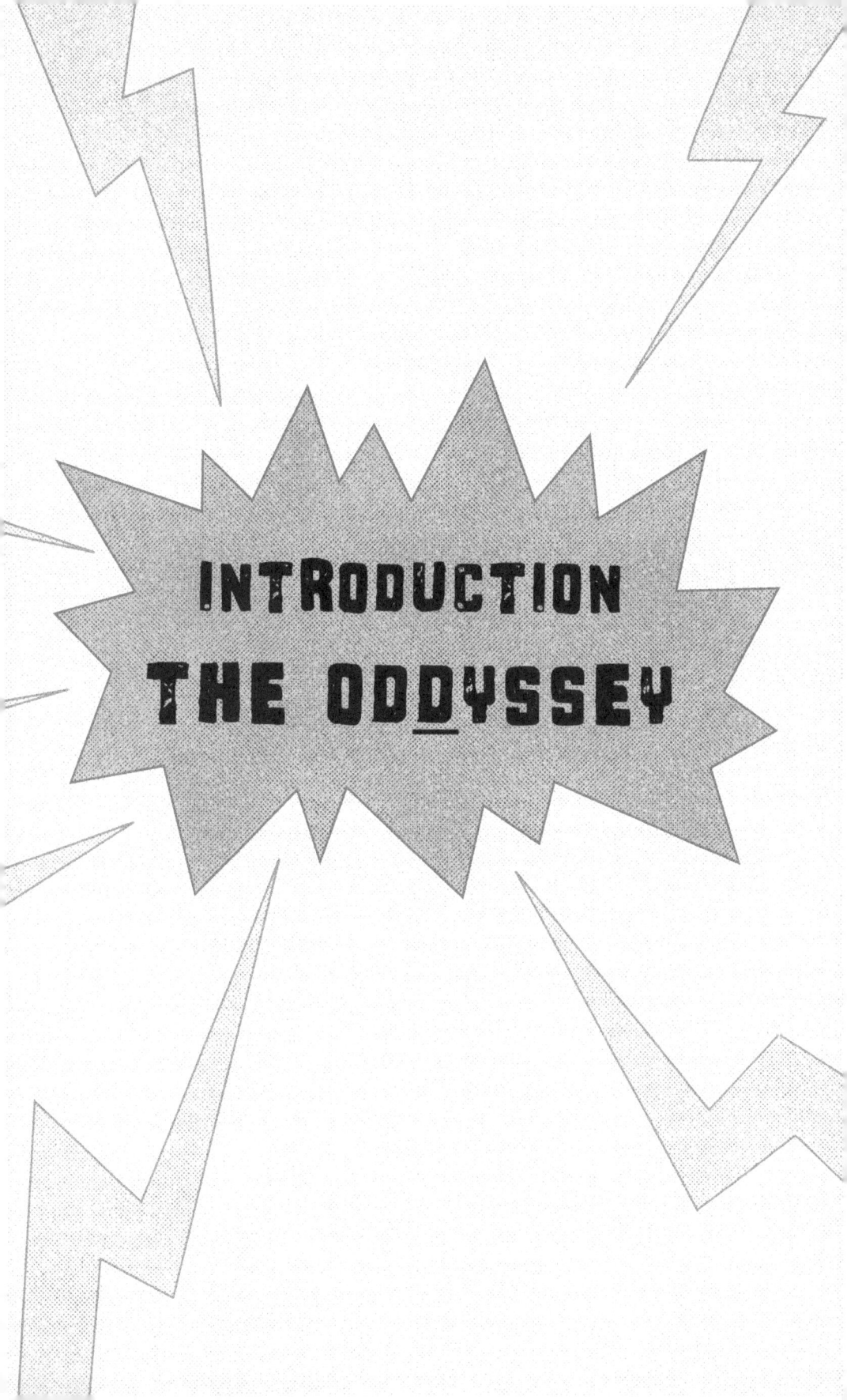

Hello, my name is Dan Schreiber: fact hunter, former co-holder of the Guinness World Records title for 'Longest Game of Keepy-Uppy with a Balloon Ever', and investigator of all **THINGS IMPOSSIBLE**.

Dan
(FACT DETECTIVE)

I am writing to you from the twenty-first century ... **OR** if you believe in the **'phantom time hypothesis'** (a weird theory that claims that nearly 300 years of history never actually happened, and that all events between the years 614 and 911 CE were just made up by a Roman Emperor and a Pope) then I am writing to you from the year **1727** ... **OR** if you believe in **'Last Thursdayism'** (which is the idea that the universe didn't begin a long time ago, but actually only started last week and that everything has just been made to look like it's been here for billions of years to trick you) then I'm writing to you from just three days since the beginning of time!

I'm afraid I can't be sure *when* I am coming to you from, but what I am sure of is *where* I am coming to you from – and that is a wooden bench in Highgate, North London. I'm here, with my **YOGIBOGEYBOOK** ready in hand, because I am attempting to do something **IMPOSSIBLE**. I am going to try to interview a ghost. That's right – a ghost! Now, this won't be the easiest ghost to make contact with, and that's because it isn't human: it's a chicken. To be precise, it's a nearly four-hundred-year-old half-plucked frozen ghost chicken. And I do not speak chickenese. Well, that's not quite true – I do know a few clucks. Thanks to a book called *How to Speak Chicken*, I can now say 'buh-dup' (hello), 'doh-doh-doh' (good night) and 'bwah! Bwaaah! Bwaaaah! Bwaaaaaahhh!' (I'm about to lay an egg!). Though I'm not fully sure when I'll get to use that last one.

But hopefully if I do spot this phantom fowl running past me, I can get its attention by speaking to it in its own language. *Did that guy just say he's about to lay an egg?* the confused chicken might think as it passes me. *I've got to see this.*

According to reports, this ghost chicken has been spotted many times by locals. Sometimes it has been seen sitting in the branches of the trees surrounding the square, and other times it has been spotted running around in continuous circles. There are even accounts of a hungry Second World War air raid warden chasing after it in an attempt to catch it for dinner.

That was a long time ago, though. I've now been sitting here for over an hour, and so far nothing. Though I must admit, I've not got high hopes, as no one has seen this chicken for a long time. And there might be a very worrying reason for that. But I'm getting ahead of myself! We'll find out more about that in chapter 2. For now, while I wait for the chicken to show up, I thought I'd fill the time by introducing myself, as well as explaining what this book is and why it's incredibly important that you should read it.

You see, right now, as you read these words, there are people all over our planet who are trying to solve **IMPOSSIBLE THINGS**. They are trying to find out if we can talk to each other using just our minds, or they are trying to make contact with aliens in distant galaxies, or they are trying to prove there are monsters roaming the

Earth and swimming in our lochs. But so far no one has 100% proven that any of these things are true. That's where you come in. Perhaps you might one day be the person who solves these mysteries and uncovers the truth. I hope you join us in the hunt, because we need all the help we can get to find the **ANSWERS TO ALL OF THE WORLD'S WEIRDEST QUESTIONS.**

- Are Venus flytraps actually aliens from another planet?
- Did dinosaurs land on the Moon 66 million years before us?
- Should doctors be giving us anti-comet medicine?
- And will a time-travelling poo one day accidentally

DESTROY ALL OF HUMANITY?

These are just some of the questions we will be tackling over the course of this book. I am going to take you on a journey into the world of the bizarre, to meet the people who are trying to get to the bottom of these questions, and most importantly I'm going to show how you too can become an Impossible Investigator.

HOW TO BECOME AN IMPOSSIBLE INVESTIGATOR

Becoming an Impossible Investigator is easy. There are just three simple rules.

1. Don't go anywhere without your YOGIBOGEYBOOK

A **YOGIBOGEYBOOK** is a special place to write down all of the weird things that you notice as you go about your day-to-day life. It's important that you jot these things down, because much like a dream, they can quickly disappear from your memory. Get yourself a book that fits in a backpack or your pocket, and make sure you log all the weird and **IMPOSSIBLE THINGS** you notice and hear about. I take my **YOGIBOGEYBOOK** with me wherever I go. It is full of odd and fantastic ideas, amazing coincidences, spooky happenings and the occasional sketch – for example, just now, I drew what I think a ghost chicken might look like.

My **YOGIBOGEYBOOK** is crammed with lists (like 'Time-travel destinations I want to go to'), diary entries (like 'Today I have travelled five hours on a train to try to spot a levitating sausage roll') and general notes (like 'Important: must remember to start training my house plant to become a police detective').

It is essential that every Impossible Investigator keeps their **YOGIBOGEYBOOK** with them at all times. All you need is an empty notebook and a pencil, and you're off.

2. Never laugh at an impossible idea, always laugh with it

I recently spoke to a man who said he believed that Adam and Eve from the Bible were not actually humans.

'What were they?' I asked.

'Garden vegetables,' he replied.

'You mean . . . like carrots?'

'More like asparagus,' he replied.

The best **IMPOSSIBLE THINGS** should make you laugh when you first hear them. Because as soon as you start taking them seriously, things go wrong. Never mock the people and the ideas that they believe in, always ask questions, and when they say something interesting, take your pencil out and write it down in your **YOGIBOGEYBOOK**.

3. Tom does not have a magical bottom

Always be cautious when investigating **IMPOSSIBLE THINGS**, because while they are fascinating and exciting, often there is a reasonable explanation. Remember: just because millions of people say they see a ghost, it doesn't make it fact. What we need is solid proof. If you're gullible, like me, you will sometimes fall for some really odd things. Like the time I believed that my friend Tom had a magical bottom. I was told Tom never needed to wipe his bum after going to the toilet. Nor did his mum, dad, sisters or brother! *Incredible*, I thought, *an entire family with magical bottoms.* For years I believed this story. Then one day, I discovered that my friends had tricked me. You see, I had believed something because it sounded so weird I wanted it to be true.

NOTE TO SELF: Remember to apologise to Tom for the many years I spent spreading the rumour that he had a magical bottom.

That's it. Stick to those three rules and you'll be fine. Anyway, I'd better wrap this introduction up now. It's very dark here in Pond Square, and a noise from the bush behind me just now was so scary I almost 'Bwah! Bwah! Bwaaah! Bwaaaahhhhed' in my pants.

CHAPTER 1
WHERE IS THE BEST PLACE TO NOT SEE A MONSTER?

Our Oddyssey begins on a crisp September afternoon – I was sitting in the passenger seat of a rental car next to my good friend Buttons, who wouldn't stop shouting **'WOO HOO!'** as we sped along the winding road that runs along the edge of one of the most mysterious lakes in the world: Scotland's Loch Ness.

Dotted around the banks of the loch were dozens of people, all of them staring out at its waters, cameras at the ready. We were all here for the same reason: to spot the infamous **Loch Ness Monster!**

The story of the Loch Ness Monster, or 'Nessie', began in the sixth century when an Irish monk called St Columba became the first person to record seeing it. According to the story, St Columba was walking along the River Ness, which flows from the northern end of the loch, when he came across a group of men burying their friend near the water. They claimed their friend had been attacked and killed by a giant monster while trying to swim across the

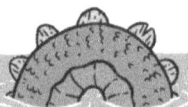

river. Curious to see the monster, St Columba decided to swim in the river himself to see if it would reappear. Well, actually, he had one of his followers do it, just in case the beast was still hungry. And it turned out it was – because as his follower paddled through the water, a *ferocious* monster rose through the surface, ready for another munch. However, before it could attack the swimmer, St Columba commanded it to leave and supposedly the monster immediately fled.

It's been over 1,400 years since that first recorded incident and we've been looking for Nessie ever since. The first thing you notice about Loch Ness is that it is waaaaay bigger than you imagined. It's massive. Locals will tell you that it is so deep, you could pop every human on Earth, all 8 billion of us, into it, and even then we wouldn't spill out on to the road (in fact, one estimate says there would be room for 72 billion more of us!). There's more water in it than in all the lakes of England and Wales combined. The perfect place for a monster to hide! I opened my **YOGIBOGEYBOOK** and started noting down some observations. **'WOO HOO!'** yelled my friend Buttons. 'I haven't been this excited since my dad told me about the time a mountain grew a face and started talking to him while he was walking through a forest.'

Before we go on, let me quickly tell you a bit about Buttons. Because that wasn't even close to being the weirdest thing he's ever said to me.

Buttons is a tall, super-intelligent yet goofy New Zealander whose real name is Leon. He got the name Buttons when he was working in a radio studio, where he had to press a lot of buttons. That's it. Buttons, like me, is also an Impossible Investigator. One **IMPOSSIBLE THING** he likes to do is sit at home, with his eyes closed, and attempt to telepathically receive that week's winning lottery numbers, which he believes are being sent to him from someone in the future. 'But who is sending you the numbers?' I asked.

'Me. I'm sending them to myself, but from a week in the future. Then once I'm done trying to receive the numbers from Future Buttons, I'll sit with the current week's lottery numbers and concentrate really hard on on sending those back in time to Past Buttons, the one who is living a week ago in the past.' He is one strange cookie.

Buttons and I have wanted to visit Loch Ness our whole lives. We've both been reading about this monster ever since we were young boys poring over books on cryptozoology.

'Cryptozoology' is the study of unknown or out-of-place animals such as Bigfoot, the Yeti, the Loch Ness Monster and then the lesser-known ones like Mothman (a terrifying humanoid moth-like creature, with big red eyes and black wings, found exclusively in West Virginia), Chupacabra (an odd dog-like character, but the size of a chimpanzee, and often depicted with a lizard's head) and the Mongolian death worm (which is said to be able to kill humans by shooting acid from its face and lightning bolts from its bottom – more on that later).

No matter where you look in this world, it seems you'll find an exciting local monster. Except, annoyingly, for the bit of Sydney, Australia, where I grew up. We had nothing! It was such a shame. Every kid should have a local monster to be terrified of. So after a lifetime of wanting to become a cryptozoologist, I was finally getting my chance. And to do this I decided to enlist the help of the second most exciting thing you can hope to find at Loch Ness besides Nessie:

A Nessie hunter!

IS THE LOCH NESS MONSTER REAL?

Sitting on a chair outside the mobile library that he calls his home, with a pair of binoculars beside him, was the man we'd come to see – the famed Nessie hunter Steve Feltham. Steve is the monster's number one believer, and he has been searching for the monster for so long he has been awarded the Guinness World Records title for the 'Longest Continuous Hunt' – **33 YEARS AND COUNTING!**

It's worth saying that Steve is a peaceful hunter, who only wants to see Nessie, not harm it. This isn't always the case with monster hunters. In America, some towns actually offer money to hunters should they be able to track down and capture Bigfoot. In fact, Bigfoot hunters in California are so keen to make a trophy out of one that years ago this caused problems during the filming of the classic Star Wars movie *Return of the Jedi*. The production team were so concerned that the actor playing Chewbacca might be mistaken for a real Bigfoot that they made sure he was always accompanied around the Californian forests by crew members in brightly coloured vests.

Steve first learned about Nessie when he was just a young boy, while out on a day trip to Loch Ness with his dad. As they drove around, Steve spotted a group of men and women sitting

in a clump, with a giant telescope next to them. 'They were the Loch Ness Phenomena Investigation Bureau,' Steve told me. 'Every summer volunteers from all over the place would come and spend their summer holidays trying to spot Nessie, and their headquarters was on this hillside. I was a seven-year-old boy watching these grown-ups trying to spot a monster in a vast loch, and I thought, *I want to do that.*'

It was fascinating talking to an actual Loch Ness monster hunter, if only because you quickly discovered that Nessie isn't quite what you thought it was.

WHAT IS THE LOCH NESS MONSTER?

No one knows what the Loch Ness Monster will turn out to be. But what Steve is absolutely convinced of is what the Loch Ness Monster isn't: the type of creature that most of us believe it to be, which is the long-necked monster called a plesiosaur that was captured in the famous 'Surgeon's Photo'.

In April 1934, the *Daily Mail* newspaper published a photograph that was reportedly taken by a doctor named Lieutenant Colonel Robert Kenneth Wilson (which is why it's called the Surgeon's Photo). The black and white photo shows a long neck popping out from the rippling water, and for many believers it became proof that the monster was real.

However, many decades after the photo was shown to the world, a man called Christian Spurling came forward to announce that the photograph was a hoax. How did he know this? It turned out he had built the fake Nessie! Spurling was the stepson of Marmaduke Wetherell, a famed big-game hunter who had been hired in 1933 by the *Daily Mail* to find the Loch Ness Monster. Wetherell had enlisted his stepson to help create a model of the monster's neck, which he did by using putty and then placing it on a toy submarine. He then asked his surgeon friend Robert Wilson to pretend he'd taken the photo and give it to the newspaper.

Since then, there have been so many new theories as to what the Loch Ness Monster, if real, might be. Some still say it's a plesiosaur, others a whale, while some say it's a species of undiscovered turtle and others think it's a giant eel. Then there are the really weird suggestions:

A RADIOACTIVE MUTANT MONSTER

According to this theory, the monster was created thanks to some fallen nuclear waste that was carried over in the wind after the Chernobyl disaster (when a reactor in a nuclear power plant exploded in the Soviet Union in 1986). Though this sounds quite mad, scientists have found the radioactive material from Chernobyl at the bottom of the loch. (An exciting thought, though this would mean the monster is only 38 years old.)

THE GHOST OF A DINOSAUR

Is it possible that Nessie is there, but can only be seen by those who can see ghosts? I was recently talking to the great explorer Colonel John Blashford-Snell, who believes this might be the case: 'It seems to me that this might be why some people can see it, while others can't.' The Colonel believes that the ability to see ghosts is a generational gift and that he inherited this ability from his parents, who were both psychic. Could Nessie spotters simply be seeing the ghost of the Loch Ness Monster?

'So what do you think it is?' I asked Steve.

'A wels catfish,' he replied. 'They are one of the largest freshwater fish in the world and can grow up to 13 feet long. And I think it might be that.'

Well, I wasn't expecting that.

DOES NESSIE KNOW WE'RE LOOKING FOR IT?

'I wonder,' I said to Steve, 'if Nessie knows we're looking for it.'

'Who knows?' Steve replied. 'There was a Nessie hunter called Ted Holiday who wrote multiple books on Nessie, and he had a theory that Nessie not only knows that we are all looking for it, but will only surface if the person looking for it doesn't have any recording devices, like a camera, or is looking the wrong way.'

Buttons and I were gutted at this idea. Would this mean we'd never catch a glimpse of Nessie? 'Well, not necessarily,' said Steve. 'Ted devised a system to outsmart Nessie. He'd stand with his back to the loch and then very suddenly spin around to catch the monster off guard. Or he'd announce loudly that he was leaving the loch and pretend to walk back to his car, but then actually walk the other way towards the loch. I'm not sure it ever worked.'

It turns out that Steve has tried every weird method there is for trying to catch a glimpse of Nessie. This is a mark of a great Impossible Investigator. Try everything, no matter how silly. And sometimes it does get silly. Like the time Steve spent a week looking for Nessie using the advice given to him by a local unicorn hunter. 'What you have to do when looking for Nessie,' she told him, 'is to not look for Nessie. Then Nessie will appear to you.' That's what she did when unicorn hunting. And so that's what Steve did: he drew up a map of where *not* to look for Nessie, went there and tried not to think about the monster. Unfortunately, Nessie didn't appear. 'Absolute waste of time,' he said.

While I was disappointed for Steve, I was absolutely flabbergasted to learn that unicorn hunters were a thing! I didn't know they existed. I quickly pulled out my **YOGIBOGEYBOOK** and added her name to the list of 'HUNTERS I ABSOLUTELY NEED TO MEET'. The Loch Ness Monster hunter was on there, but now I could cross that one off.

EXTRACT FROM THE YOGIBOGEYBOOK #1

HUNTERS I ABSOLUTELY NEED TO MEET

1. ELF HUNTER – Where: Iceland

Reason: So many people there believe in elves! (Or huldufólk, as they call them.) It is said that the creatures mostly live in rocks and exist in a parallel world where they can make themselves visible to us at will. In Iceland some people take the idea of elves so seriously that it can even affect things like construction plans. For example, if a new road is being built through an area where it is believed an elf is living, they will sometimes delay the project until the elf is relocated. One Icelandic resident even told me that the elves had once warned his parents not to sleep in their bed during a storm, and thank goodness they didn't, because a beam collapsed on their bed that night. His mum was pregnant with him at the time, and he believes it is the reason he is alive today. The elves saved his life!

2. YETI HUNTER – Where: Bhutan

Reason: Not only do many people in Bhutan believe in the Yeti, but a former king of Bhutan, Jigme Singye Wangchuck, believed in it so much he even had his own royal Yeti hunter – a man called Dasho Benji who, when he wasn't leading Yeti expeditions, also doubled as the king's basketball coach. Benji's job was to look after the Yeti sanctuary. Deep in the forests of Bhutan you will find the Sakteng Wildlife Sanctuary, where the king decreed that the preservation of the mythical Yeti would take place. And it is huge – so big, in fact, that the park could fit all of Manchester, Belfast, Edinburgh, Plymouth, Cardiff and Nottingham combined into it. So it's no wonder that Benji hasn't ever actually seen a Yeti – the park is humongous! It also doesn't help that, according to local legend, Yetis can apparently turn themselves invisible when they want and take their feet off their legs and put them on backwards to confuse hunters. So, if you're ever following some Yeti footprints, remember that they might have turned their feet around and you could be walking away from them!

3. MONGOLIAN DEATH WORM HUNTER
– Where: Gobi Desert

Reason: In the far reaches of Mongolia's Gobi Desert there is said to be a terrifying and deadly worm. The Mongolian death worm is thought to have killed many people by either spraying acid from its face or shooting lightning bolts from its bum. This was first reported by the explorer Roy Chapman Andrews (many people think he was the inspiration for Indiana Jones). Chapman had heard about the worm from locals when he was hunting for dinosaur fossils in Mongolia in 1922. He never met the worm, but he did collect numerous descriptions of it, including from the then Prime Minister Damdinbazar: 'It is shaped like a sausage about 2 feet long, has no head nor legs and it is so poisonous that merely to touch it means instant death. It lives in the most desolate parts of the Gobi Desert.'

Several explorers have since tried to find the death worm, including cryptozoologist Ivan Mackerle, who thought he could lure the worm out of hiding by using a 'thumping machine' on the Gobi Desert floor and blowing up the sand with dynamite. He was wrong, and he didn't find the deadly worm.

4. MOOSE HUNTER – Where: New Zealand

Reason: Cryptozoology is not just about 'make-believe' monsters and strange sightings; it's also about regular animals that pop up where people think they aren't meant to be. Like a wels catfish in Loch Ness, or sightings of 'big cats' like the many reports of leopards and panthers in the UK. So you can imagine how excited I was to recently discover that for over 50 years now, a man called Ken Tustin, author of *A (Nearly) Complete History of the Moose in New Zealand*, has been looking for moose in New Zealand, even though everyone agrees there are no moose in New Zealand.

Or are there? There did used to be a herd of moose there. They were introduced into New Zealand's Fiordland National Park in 1910 for hunting, but unfortunately didn't adapt to their new home and were suspected to have completely died out in the mid 1900s. But then, in 1952, a moose was caught on camera! It's the only photo of a moose in the park, but there have been the occasional reports of sightings since, and an antler was found in 1972. In the early 2000s, scientists tested some DNA collected from the park that showed they could still exist there, however Ken is still yet to prove their existence. Curiously, if he does ever see one, he says he won't ruin the moment by taking a photo if it. Which means no one will believe him even if he does find one!

5. THE LOCH NESS MONSTER HUNTER

As the day ended, we thanked Steve for his time and promised to stay in contact. I walked to the shore and quickly tried out Ted Holiday's method of facing away from the loch and then very quickly spinning around to see if I could catch Nessie. But there was nothing except for a few swimmers in the distance. *I wonder if they have monster insurance*, I thought. This is something that has been offered in the past to swimmers taking part in triathlons in the loch. Largely done as a joke no doubt, but the swimmers were genuinely insured for over a million pounds in case they were bitten by Nessie.

Meeting the Nessie hunter had been a brilliant experience, but I couldn't help but feel disappointed that I hadn't grown up with a local monster or monster hunter to believe in. 'Are you so sure about that?' asked Steve. 'I wouldn't be. There are monsters everywhere. Maybe you just need to look harder.'

I decided to do some digging in my hometown of Sydney, Australia.

YET(I) TO FIND A MONSTER

TWO YEARS LATER . . .

It was a hot summer's day in Sydney, I was back home at my family house and my phone was ringing. 'Hello?'

'WOO HOO! It's me, Buttons.'

He had just landed in Sydney and was coming to see me. I was very excited about this. I hadn't seen Buttons in a while, but more importantly, since I last saw him I had made an amazing discovery that I couldn't wait to show him.

As soon as Buttons arrived, I hurried him back into the car for a 20 minute journey to Narrabeen Lagoon.

'Why are we here?' Buttons asked as he stepped out of the car.

'I wanted to show you this,' I said, handing him a newspaper article I had found just a few days before. **'I'VE FOUND MY MONSTER.'**

It was here, at 1.15 p.m. on 3 April 1968, that a woman named Mrs Mabel Walsh reported seeing a tiny elephant-like creature walk out of the lake on its hind legs and then dart off into the bush. Her description of it was incredible.

This is what she told Australia's *Daily Telegraph* a few days after the sighting: '*It was a bit over 4 feet tall, with dark grey, tough leathery skin, like an elephant's. It had small front legs and walked on its hind legs, which were thick and round like an elephant's . . . I didn't notice a tail or ears, but it had small eyes and smaller front legs or arms. Its head reminded me of an anteater's. Its trunk was rigid, squared off at the end and stuck down and out at an angle.*' Unfortunately, she had been taking her nephew to the airport at the time, so she wasn't able to stop and investigate. She and her husband did later return to the lagoon to look for the monster, but had no luck.

The next sighting of the Narrabeen Lagoon Monster was in 1971, by two fishermen who briefly saw the elephant humanoid out on the lagoon. But ever since then, nothing. Where did the monster go?

Buttons and I now stood on the lip of Narrabeen Lagoon, looking out at it. Steve Feltham was right. It turns out I *did* have a local monster growing up – it was just 20 minutes away and I had no idea.

'Well, what shall we call it?' asked Buttons.

'Narrie,' I replied. In honour of its cousin Nessie.

As we continued to look, it occurred to me that being an Impossible Investigator is often about travelling long distances to places like Loch Ness to not see the monster. Sure, you hope you'll see it. But you know that a sighting is rare, and really you'll just be staring at the water for hours, not seeing it. And there's something beautiful about that.

With excitement I realised that we were possibly the first people in decades to actively *not* see Narrie. To be looking out at this body of water and *not* seeing the monster said to be living in it. And maybe in time, thousands more people would start coming here to *not* see Narrie too. Until one day, maybe someone will see it.

'Pretty amazing,' I said. 'In fact, I think it might be the best thing I've ever *not* seen.'

'Woo hoo,' agreed Buttons.

CHAPTER 2
DO GHOSTS EVER GET BORED OF HAUNTING US?

One of the most exciting areas for an Impossible Investigator to explore is the world of the paranormal. For as long as I can remember, I have been logging great ghost stories in my **YOGIBOGEYBOOK**. Some are interesting, some are scary and some seem impossible. I'd now like to present you with the scariest, most convincing story I've ever known. Buckle up, it's time for a ghost story . . .

NIGHT AT THE IMPOSSIBLE HOTEL

The hotel itself wasn't scary to look at from the outside. It wasn't a giant gothic castle with terrifying stone statues of devilish dragons perched on its sides, and it wasn't a futuristic silver dome built by an evil billionaire. No, this impossible hotel was a Holiday Inn. No different to the ones you get in places like Bolton or Glasgow. But what made this particular Holiday Inn curious was its location – it was built on the side of a Himalayan mountain in Tibet. And in the autumn of 1990, something terrifying was about to happen.

Earlier that summer, a young Australian called Dean and his fiancée, Bettina, walked through the hotel's front doors to begin a new life as hotel staff. They had uprooted their lives from a sunny beachside town in Sydney to come to the icy mountains, and the moment they arrived they knew that everything was going to change. The food, for example, was going to take some getting used to – everything on the hotel menu seemed to be made from yak. There was yak butter, yak cheese, yak burgers and therefore yak cheeseburgers. The only other option on the menu was salmon, but the couple decided to avoid that particular dish after learning that one of the local burial traditions involved dropping dead humans into the salmon ponds to feed the fish.

All was going well at the hotel for Dean and Bettina, until they hit their first winter. The snow was piled so high that it made getting to the hotel virtually impossible, so they had hardly any guests. One night, Dean and Bettina were in their room when they heard a noise coming from the room above, on the third floor –

– it sounded like a child jumping off the bed on to the floor, over and over. Knowing the rooms above them weren't occupied, the couple suspected that some of the hotel staff must have sneaked into it, or perhaps some new guests had unexpectedly arrived. Either way, the constant thumping above annoyed them. Dean called reception and asked who was in the room above. 'No one' came the reply. The room was completely unoccupied.

continued the sounds.

Eventually, Dean decided to go and investigate. Arming himself with an umbrella, he went upstairs. But when he got there the noise had stopped. He waited outside to see if it would begin again, but he heard nothing. Just as he was about to head back down, Bettina appeared, a look of confusion on her face. She was also armed with an umbrella. 'Why haven't you told them to be quiet?' she asked. 'The noise hasn't stopped since you left.' Suddenly realising there might be a ghost in the room, they ran back down to the second floor bedroom and hid beneath the blankets of their bed, shaking with fear.

THUMP THUMP THUMP.

The next morning, Dean and Bettina mentioned the odd knocking noise to the only other guests staying on their side of the hotel. 'No, we didn't hear any thumping,' said the couple who were staying on the third floor. *Phew*, thought Dean and Bettina. 'But we did hear a child crying as it ran up and down the corridor.' Dean and Bettina froze in terror. There was no child in the hotel that night. Curious to find out if anyone else had experienced anything odd, Dean spoke to one of the hotel's secretaries. She admitted that she had recently got a call from an old lady who was crying hysterically and asking where her baby was, before quickly hanging up. As she headed down to reception to report the call to the front desk, she heard a child crying in the hall, but she found no one there. It was then that Dean realised he was living in a haunted hotel! Who was the crying child? Who was the old lady?

A year later, some real children arrived at the hotel – Dean's nephew and niece, who had come to visit with their parents and another family of friends. Dean had hesitated about telling any of them about the hauntings, in case it might put them off coming, and besides, there hadn't been any weird supernatural events for a while now. They were all given a room . . . on the third floor.

All was well until the fourth night of their stay, when, as the parents were enjoying dinner (mainly by avoiding the salmon) in the restaurant on the ground level, the children went up to play in their room.

As Dean entertained his guests, his sister-in-law mentioned that she'd had trouble sleeping the night before. There had been a consistent tapping against her bedroom window. It must have been a tree branch, she thought. Dean's face went white. He confessed that there were no trees outside the bedroom window, and, left with no option, he came clean and explained all the paranormal activities in the hotel.

After listening intently, the mum realised that if something was tapping on the window, it might still be there, and the children were in that very room now – all alone. They all immediately abandoned their yak steaks and headed up to room 318. As the elevator door opened to the third floor, Dean heard children screaming. They dashed to the room and discovered the youngest and only girl of the group sitting by herself at the table next to the window. The four boys were balled up in the corner, shaking with fear, and in front of them was a broken glass.

'What's happened?' asked Dean. Trembling, the girl's brother explained how his sister had suddenly started acting weird and said that she was going to levitate a glass of water by just staring at it. The boys encouraged her to give it a go, but after her initial attempt failed, they resumed playing. All except her brother, who kept an eye on her, noticing that she was still acting strangely. She was stuck, trance-like, staring at the glass when, suddenly, the glass lifted into the air on its own, remained hanging a few feet above the table for a few seconds, and then shattered into hundreds of tiny pieces.

The mother quickly gathered the children and refused to return to the third floor for the rest of the stay.

Is this story true? Did the impossible really happen? It's hard to say. Stories like this appear in countless volumes of ghost books or are told to you by a friend who says it's true and that it happened to their mum's best friend's dentist's dad's parrot, but there's often very little evidence to show they're true. This story is different, however. I can promise you that. Because, you see, the man who was running the hotel was my uncle Dean Schreiber, the girl by the window was my sister, Chyna, and the boy who saw the glass lift into the air that night in the hotel . . . was me.

WE'RE GOING ON A GHOST HUNT

Many years later, I still have no idea what happened that night in the Tibetan hotel. It must have had a huge impact, though, as I've been chasing ghosts ever since, and recently I found myself sitting on a bench on a cold and wet Sunday morning at Yeovil Junction train station, looking to make contact with yet another curious ghost. I've tried multiple times to meet a ghost since that Tibetan trip, but with no luck. My **YOGIBOGEYBOOK** is jam-packed with curious ghosts to check out.

EXTRACT FROM THE YOGIBOGEYBOOK #2

LIST OF GHOSTS TO VISIT

- [x] **GHOST OF FROZEN CHICKEN**
  Highgate Pond Square, London
  Notes: Attempted to make contact with the ghostly chicken but saw nothing. Heard a noise in the bush and was so scared I almost laid an egg

- [ ] **LEVITATING SAUSAGE ROLL**
  The buffet at Yeovil Junction train station café

- [ ] **HAUNTED BAG OF SOOT**
  Walshes Road, Jarvis Brook

I hoped I would get to tick another box on that list when I investigated the haunted café at Yeovil Junction train station. The café is said to be haunted by a woman called Molly, who used to work at the station. Apparently, Molly likes to mess with the cutlery: she moves forks around and lifts stuff into the air. So I've come to try to spot her levitating something, like a sausage roll.

Getting here involved a 5 hour Sunday train ride for me, but I knew it would be worth it. It was only when I arrived that I realised I'd made a huge mistake. The café wasn't open. (A lesson for the Impossible Investigator – always check the opening hours!) It was only open Monday to Saturday, and despite how much I pleaded with the station manager, he wouldn't let me in. Not even to see a flying sausage roll! I peered through the café window instead, but with the lights off inside it was hard to make out much. Maybe ghosts don't work on Sundays. And so I feel I can't quite tick that box in my **YOGIBOGEYBOOK**.

NOTE TO SELF: Find out what ghosts get up to on weekends.

Maybe I will have better luck hunting my next ghost in the village of Jarvis Brook, in Sussex, where a hill is thought to be haunted by a giant bag of soot. I was surprised enough that there was such a thing as a ghost animal – I had thought it was just humans that became ghosts – but a ghost bag of black, powdery burnt wood is very exciting. There are a few accounts of this haunting, including one about a blacksmith who supposedly went up the hill specifically to prove that the ghostly soot didn't exist, only to be found moments later dashing back down the hill, followed in hot pursuit by a big raging bag of the stuff!

With time to spare at Yeovil station, I started to wonder if my experience at the haunted hotel is what led me to become an Impossible Investigator. It's my own personal **IMPOSSIBLE THING**. Who was the old grandma calling on the phone, looking for a missing child? Was it a granny ghost that possessed my sister, Chyna, making her levitate the glass with her eyes? Or, like Matilda in the Roald Dahl book, did Chyna just use her own mind to levitate the glass herself? Or did I just imagine it all?

I realised I hadn't asked my sister about it in years. I got my phone out and messaged her.

DAN: Hey sis, bit of a weird question, but do you remember lifting a glass with your mind and then shattering it into pieces while it was hanging in the air?

My phone pinged minutes later with a reply:

> **CHYNA:** Yes, 100%. I watched it lift off the table!

> **DAN:** Thanks.

> **CHYNA:** What you up to?

> **DAN:** Just sitting at a train station trying to spot a floating sausage roll.

> **CHYNA:** OK. Have fun.

I put my phone away. So she did remember! But did it happen? Here's the weird thing: despite witnessing it, I'm not sure I believe it. **'WHHHHHHAAAAAAAT???????'** I can almost hear the Tibetan ghost scream from thousands of miles away. And, of course, it should be angry. It's probably sitting with its other poltergeist friends saying, 'He doesn't believe in me? What more do I have to do? I smashed a glass in mid-air in front of this kid, and he thinks science will explain it? I give up!'

But it's true. I don't know if I believe in ghosts. And that must be so frustrating for ghosts, if they're real, having people like me not believe in them. And this lack of belief might be a greater problem than we all realise.

DO GHOSTS GET ANGRY WHEN SOMEONE DOESN'T BELIEVE IN THEM?

It turns out they do. In fact, a few years ago, a man who was reported to be Poland's only officially registered ghost hunter hit the headlines with what he claimed was a very worrying discovery:

GHOSTS ARE THREATENING TO QUIT HAUNTING US!

According to Piter Shalkevitz, the Polish ghost hunter, too many of us have turned into non-believers. As a result, he believes that ghosts are finding it too frustrating to haunt us any more. What's the point if no one is going to believe in them? They've basically said, 'If you're going to have that attitude, we won't bother haunting you any more.'

Piter wanted to set up an international poll so that everyone in the world would answer the question **'DO YOU BELIEVE IN GHOSTS?'** with a yes or no. He would then know how many believers there are and could show it to the ghosts to convince them to continue to haunt us and not go on strike. Did he ever get round to doing it? He didn't need to in the end. Apparently, the Polish ghosts were so happy with all the press coverage they got from their threat (they made international news!) that reports of hauntings shot back up again.

GHOSTS ON STRIKE

Safe in this knowledge, Piter has since quit hunting ghosts to become an exorcist. (An exorcist is like a plumber for demons. Just as a plumber will come to remove something blocking your toilet, an exorcist will remove a blockage in your body. But instead of removing something like clogged toilet paper from the pipe, they believe they can remove an evil spirit from your soul.)

WHO WERE THE FIRST GHOSTS?

If Piter is right about ghosts disappearing, we would be getting rid of some of the most important companions humans have ever had. Ghosts have always been with us. There are examples of them that date back right to the very beginning of recorded history. One person who knows all about them is my friend Dr Irving Finkel. Irving works at the British Museum and is the assistant keeper of the Sumerian and Babylonian collections. The Sumerians and Babylonians were two great civilisations from the Middle East. It was through these cultures that the first ever writing emerged.

'Did you know you're standing in the oldest library in the world?' Irving asked me as we stood in the back rooms of the museum. It didn't feel very old. It looked very modern. But he was right. Libraries aren't old because of their shelves; they are old because of the books they have on those shelves. And the 'books' in this library, all 130,000 of them, were up to 5,000 years old. So old that they pre-date actual books. They are instead all stories and facts pressed on to tiny tablets of clay, called cuneiform tablets. The language they are written in is extinct. But Irving knows how to read them.

'Have you ever seen a ghost, Irving?' I asked.

'Do you know, I'm rather sad to say I haven't. Though I would love to. This library apparently has a ghost. Many have seen it, but not me. Not for want of trying. I've often sat alone in the dark when everyone has gone home, quietly eating a sandwich, waiting for one to appear, but no such luck so far.'

I told Irving about the possible retirement plan ghosts are threatening us with, and Irving seemed very worried by it. 'So many of the tablets here tell of spells of how to deal with ghosts, or diagnose what kind of ghost lives in your house, or move a ghost to a new home. They knew everything about ghosts and it was a part of their day-to-day lives. Look around you – we can't lose our ghosts, this room is an overwhelming testimony to the fact that ghosts are a part of a human belief system, and have been since the beginning of time.'

'I'd sure love to see one,' I said to Irving.

'Me too. And if I ever find one, you'll be the first person I call!'

WHERE'S THE MOST HAUNTED PLACE IN THE UK?

Unlike Poland, the UK has never had any shortage of ghosts. And if you want to see one, your best bet is probably a village called Pluckley. It even has a Guinness World Records title for 'Most Haunted Village'. Or at least it did. When I looked into it, I discovered that the record had been cancelled. *Oh no, the ghosts will be furious*, I thought, searching the news archives for headlines like 'Pluckley ghosts threaten to go on strike!' Luckily, I couldn't find any. Why was their record revoked? Fortunately, I was able to message someone who would know – a fellow Impossible Investigator: Craig Glenday, the editor-in-chief of Guinness World Records.

'Aww. Sorry about that,' Craig wrote back. 'It was deactivated, along with most other "most haunted" records! It's very difficult to prove any of these ghostly "records", of course!'

No ghosts in the Guinness World Records? That wasn't right. And for the first time since I was a kid, I was scared of ghosts again . . . scared of them leaving us.

Even if you don't believe in ghosts, there are so many reasons to keep them. I started to make a list in my **YOGIBOGEYBOOK** to remind myself about the reasons.

EXTRACT FROM THE YOGIBOGEYBOOK #3

THE REASONS WE NEED GHOSTS

1. THEY CAN MAKE YOU RICH!

Having a ghost in the house isn't always a bad thing. In fact, it can lead to a lot of money. Some people make money off their haunted houses, like 30 East Drive in Pontefract. It's one of the most famous haunted houses in the UK, said to be home to a poltergeist known as 'the black monk of Pontefract', because of the long black robes he wears. He also goes by 'Fred' – named so by the family who first discovered him, presumably because saying 'the black monk of Pontefract' over and over got really annoying and they just needed something shorter.

The house has become a huge attraction to those who love ghost experiences and can be hired out to rent. And reading the reviews from people who have stayed there is bizarre: 'had an amazing night, glasses getting thrown off tables, tables tipping on their own, slept over and was scared the whole time' and then another by someone who described a bottle of water hitting their face, a Bible hitting their stomach and a flying crucifix hitting their head. They gave it five stars!

2. THEY ARE GOOD FOR YOUR HEALTH

According to science, watching a scary movie can burn as many calories as doing some exercise! So if you go to the cinema and eat a chocolate bar and get scared enough, you will possibly burn off the bar by the time you've finished the movie. Perhaps every gym should have a ghost. Do some weightlifting, run on a treadmill, then get terrified by a poltergeist who's trying to throw a dumbbell at your head.

3. THEY CAN HELP YOUR FAVOURITE SPORTS TEAM WIN

In 2014, several England cricket players had to move rooms in their hotel because weird things were happening that kept them up at night and left them knackered the next day.

Bowler Stuart Broad told newspapers: 'It was so hot in the room I just couldn't sleep. All of a sudden, the taps in the bathroom came on for no reason. I turned the lights on, and the taps turned themselves off. Then when I switched the lights off again, the taps came on. It was very weird. It really freaked me out.'

A fear of ghosts seems to run in the blood of English cricketers. Former England player and *Top Gear* host Freddie Flintoff got in trouble thanks to his fear of ghosts. He was staying in Zimbabwe with his team when one of the players, Mal Loye, started telling ghost stories which freaked Flintoff out so much he ended up too scared to sleep alone. Freddie made sure he was sharing a room with another cricketer, Vikram Solanki – his logic being that because Vikram was religious, maybe the ghosts would leave him alone. He got barely any sleep that night. As a result, Freddie was 15 minutes late to training and fined £2,000 for it. Not only that, but according to Flintoff, once he had explained who told them the scary stories, Loye was fined thousands of pounds too!

Over in America, some NBA stars claim they're petrified of certain hotels because of the ghosts. One such hotel is called The Skirvin, and it is supposedly haunted by the ghost of a woman called Effie on the tenth floor.

The story goes that Effie died in the hotel and has been haunting it ever since. Multiple basketball players have reported encounters, including New York Knicks player Eddy Curry, who, like Flintoff, had to move into a different room and sleep with a teammate so that he could escape Effie.

The moral is, pop your rivals into a haunted hotel the night before a big game, and they'll be exhausted from hiding awake under their blankets all night and won't perform their best in the game!

THE OLDEST GHOST ON EARTH

A few months after my trip to the British Museum, I received a call from Irving Finkel: 'Good news, I found you a ghost to meet. Get back to the museum as soon as possible!'

Irving told me about the ghost, and I couldn't have been more excited. 'I'm coming,' I said, and then had a thought. 'Wait, I just need to make a phone call. Can I bring a friend?'

A few days later I found myself staring at a 2,500-year-old Babylonian clay tablet, featuring a drawing of an elderly male ghost being walked into the underworld by a female figure. 'There it is!' said Irving. 'Not only does this cuneiform tablet have a ghost drawn on it, but it is the oldest depiction of a ghost ever to be drawn. What you're looking at is the oldest recorded ghost on Earth!'

In the drawing the ghost has its hands tied and is being walked into the underworld. I was gobsmacked and so was the man standing next to me, Craig Glenday of the Guinness World Records. Craig had a camera in one hand and something very special in the other – a certificate for the ghost, to award it the title for the **'OLDEST DEPICTION OF A GHOST'**.

'Congratulations,' I said under my breath to any ghosts that might have been watching us. 'A ghost just made it back into the Guinness World Records.' Having spent years trying to meet another ghost, I'd finally done it. And it didn't require me to believe or disbelieve in it.

DEAN'S OTHER HAUNTING

It was Saturday night in Sydney, not long after my day at Narrabeen Lagoon in search of Narrie, when I decided to pay a visit to my uncle Dean and auntie Bettina. They had left Tibet many years ago and now lived back in Australia. I wanted to talk to my uncle about what happened that night in Tibet.

'So how about the ghost in that hotel and that old granny on the phone. Did you ever work out who she was?' I asked.

'We didn't, but we still talk about it,' Dean replied.

'Probably the scariest thing you ever experienced, I bet?'

'No,' he said with a shiver. 'There was another ghost, and this one was truly terrifying.'

I took out my **YOGIBOGEYBOOK** and started taking notes as Dean told me the story. Many years after Dean and Bettina left Tibet, they moved to Singapore and had two children, Ash and Lucas. They found a nice place to live, but when they moved in Dean sensed something odd about the house. Particularly the staircase. He couldn't put his finger on what it was, but there was something weird about that spot.

One day, Dean was sitting with his back to the landing, when out of the corner of his eye he saw a little boy run down the stairs. Turning around, he expected to see his three-year-old son, Lucas. But no one was there. *It must be my mind playing tricks,* thought Dean. But it happened again and again, the boy becoming clearer to Dean with each sighting. A young boy who looked exactly like his own three-year-old would run on the stairs. Not wanting to scare anyone in the house, Dean kept it to himself.

One night Dean and Bettina were sitting on the landing when Dean spotted the boy again in the corner of his eye. He tried to ignore it, as he usually did, when Bettina said, 'You see it too, don't you?'

Before she could say anything else, Dean shouted, 'Wait! Don't speak! Let's both write down what we think we just saw and show it to each other.'

This, by the way, is an excellent way for all Impossible Investigators to work out if someone else has seen the same **IMPOSSIBLE THING**. If there are two or more people present, always write down what happened before saying what happened out loud.

When they revealed what they thought they had just seen, each of them had written: small child, blond, red/orange T-shirt.

They were terrified.

Then, one night when Dean and Bettina were in bed, chatting to each other in the dark, Lucas opened the door and walked to the bed. Bettina lifted the sheet to let Lucas in. He got in. A few moments later, there was a knock at the door. It was Lucas: 'Can I come to bed with you?' Dean and Bettina freaked out. Who had jumped into bed with them just a few moments before? They looked under the sheets, but no one was to be found.

The last straw came one night when Lucas fell on to the floor and started moving weirdly.

'What are you doing?' Dean asked him.

And he said, 'I am a ghost!'

'But there's no such thing as a ghost.'

'Yes, there is,' he replied and he turned and pointed to the staircase and said, 'Like the boy.'

Dean immediately picked him up, left the house, booked a hotel room, and put the house up for sale.

The house they now live in in Sydney is not haunted. Having finished his tale, I closed my **YOGIBOGEYBOOK** and Dean and I walked to the kitchen to get a drink from the fridge. I suppose I'll never know what happened in Tibet all those years ago. The crying child, the old lady, I was at a dead end. It was the end of the story. It was then, as I looked at their fridge door, I noticed that they had a load of magnetic alphabet letters on there. Some of them had been used to spell 'dean and bettina' and, on a row below, 'lucas' and 'ash'. I don't why, but I started playing with the letters to see if I could make some other words. And that's when I saw it. Using the three words 'dean', 'and' and 'bettina', I jumbled them up and eventually found myself staring at three new words. I had spelled out something that sent a shiver through my spine: 'dead tibetan nan'.

CHAPTER 3
ARE ROCK STARS SECRETLY ALIENS?

When I was a young boy, my dad used to tell me about an alien living on Earth who was hiding in plain sight. Everyone suspected he was an alien, but no one could prove it. He had arrived on our planet, integrated himself into our society and eventually became one of the most famous singers in the world. His name was David Bowie. Dad said you could tell he was an alien because when he was putting together his human-body disguise, he got everything right except the colours of his eyes. One was blue and one was brown. And then there were the songs he wrote: 'Life on Mars?', 'Loving the Alien', 'Space Oddity', 'Starman'. It's like he wasn't even trying to hide it. He was even cast in a movie called *The Man Who Fell to Earth* in which he **PLAYED AN ALIEN WHO WAS TRICKING HUMANS INTO THINKING HE WAS A NORMAL PERSON**. 'Could he be any more obvious?!' my dad said.

When I was a bit older, I realised I had been lied to. 'Dad! David Bowie's not an alien! I just read a book that told me the reason he had one brown and one blue eye is because of a fight he had with his best friends at school when he was young.'

'Ah, a clever cover story for an alien from Mars, don't you think?' said my dad.

'He wasn't from Mars, Dad! He was from London. And his eyes weren't even different colours,' I continued. 'The incident at school just made one pupil look bigger, giving the impression it was a different colour.'

'Yeah, yeah, yeah,' said Dad. 'You'll see one day that I'm right. He's a Martian, alright.'

IS THERE LIFE ON MARS?

In August of 1924, a peculiar request was issued by the US government: everyone with a radio receiver in America was to spend 36 hours listening out for messages being sent to Earth from aliens on Mars.

According to astronomers, Mars was going to be the closest to Earth that it had been for a long time, and if there was intelligent life living there, they might use this as an opportunity to communicate by radio. So on this 'National Radio Silence Day', the nation was asked to do their bit by listening out for the aliens for 5 minutes on the hour, every hour, for 36 hours. The US Navy even commissioned inventor Charles Francis Jenkins and astronomer David Peck Todd to create a special device to record the messages (which they did – the snappily titled 'radio photo message continuous transmission machine'), while also issuing out a command to all their operators to listen out specifically for Martian messages, even assigning a translator to decipher any messages received. The radio operators listened attentively for anything that might come through. Nothing did, though.

This may seem odd to us now, but for a long time many people believed Mars had aliens living on it. There was once even a prize created by a Parisian high-society woman named Clara Gouget Guzman, who in her will left 100,000 francs (just over £500,000 in today's money) to be awarded to the first person to make contact with aliens. It had one condition: the winner couldn't be someone who had made contact with a Martian, because Clara was already convinced that Martians existed!

There have been many attempts to make contact with the aliens on Mars over the years. One plan was to coat the Eiffel Tower in mirrors, so that it could beam light towards Mars (like a morse code message).

This idea came from a man known as Mr A. Mercier, who speculated about some mysterious lights that had been observed on the surface Mars. Could it be, wondered Mercier, that these lights were in fact a response message to the giant lights that had briefly been set up on the Eiffel Tower in 1889? Had the Martians seen those lights and thought we were trying to communicate? Mercier proposed that a permanent night-time communication tower be built for the Martians – by coating the Eiffel Tower in mirrors, so that at sunset they could be angled to beam the sunlight towards Mars. And just to make sure the aliens knew that this wasn't a natural phenomenon, a giant screen would be attached to the top of the Eiffel Tower to occasionally give it cover and break up the light (like a Morse Code message). Mercier reckoned this would cost about 50,000 francs to achieve and started collecting funds. However, the mirrors of the Eiffel Tower were never built.

Another French inventor, Charles Cros, believed that the mystery lights that had been seen on Mars were from large Martian cities, and he also wanted to use giant mirrors to make contact with them. However, instead of using the light as a sort of flashing mode of communication, Cros wanted to use the beam of directed sunlight to physically burn a message into the surface of the planet. Cros's idea of burning a message into the surface of Mars never happened. It's probably good it didn't, because if there were any Martians living there, I doubt they would have appreciated having giant words like **'WE COME IN PEACE'** burning through their walls and destroying their homes.

THE FIRST FLYING SAUCERS

'Hey, Dan.' It was Dad on the phone. 'Guess what? Remember when you were young I told you that David Bowie was an alien? New evidence has just come in!'

'Oh yeah?' I said excitedly, hoping that Dad had some exciting revelations to share.

'It's a song from his new album – it's called "Born in a UFO".'

'Dad, that's not proof.'

'I know that, but I did some research. Do you know when David Bowie was born?'

'No,' I said, confused as to where this was going.

'1947! The same year as the first ever major reporting of a UFO!'

Hang on, Dan! I can hear you yelling. *Are you saying that the first time anyone claimed aliens were visiting us was in 1947???*

Calm down. Not at all. There have been plenty of alien sightings before then. Like the bizarre record we have from the twelfth century that tells of two green children who mysteriously appeared in the village of Woolpit in Suffolk. According to the writing of a man called Ralph of Coggeshall, the children arrived confused and speaking a language unknown to anyone. Sir Richard de Calne took them in and attempted to feed them, but instead watched as they ate food directly out of the ground in his vegetable garden. As time went on, he taught them English and they told him they came from a land called St Martin. Who these green children were remains a mystery to this day. But I can't help but note how suspiciously close the words St Martin and Martian are to each other.

So yes, history is littered with alien encounters, but it wasn't until 1947 that the idea of flying saucers properly came to our attention.

On 24 June 1947, Kenneth Arnold was flying in his plane over Mount Rainier in Washington, USA, when suddenly he saw something in the sky. Or rather, he saw nine somethings in the sky. Nine shining objects, all flying in weird, erratic formations. Each looked to be approximately 100 feet wide, shaped like a giant circle and travelling at around 1,200 miles per hour. That's much faster than any plane at the time could fly, and is still double the speed of any commercial airline flying today. When he landed, Arnold reported this UFO (unidentified flying object). Arnold instantly became world famous, and he would go on to say that he saw many more UFOs in his life – including a transparent one that acted like a giant jellyfish.

Arnold's experience sparked off a whole wave of sightings, with over 800 UFOs eventually being reported in the USA in the wake of his story. And then the BIG alien spaceship moment happened a few months later, possibly the most famous claim of a UFO crash on Earth ever. It was called the Roswell incident.

THE ROSWELL INCIDENT

'The Roswell incident also happened in 1947!' said Dad. 'The same year that Bowie was born! It was all happening!'

The Roswell incident was huge. Sure, everyone was seeing UFOs in the sky, but now someone had reported that a UFO had actually crashed on Earth and that the aliens had been recovered.

Here are a few things you need to know about the Roswell crash.

> It didn't happen in Roswell; it happened closer to the neighbouring town of Corona. (No, not the coronavirus!) It's only called Roswell because the emergency services that responded to the call of a crashed vehicle were from Roswell and that is where the debris was moved to.
>
> An astronaut who had landed on the Moon, Edgar Mitchell, was from Roswell, and he believed that the incident was real.
>
> Another notable celebrity from Roswell is the original actor who played the Red Power Ranger. This is not important or relevant. I just thought you should know that.

'So you're saying Bowie's new song is a confession that he is an alien?' I asked.

'Correct!' said Dad.

'I don't think so, Dad.'

'OK, I thought you might say that. So, I've found another angle. Maybe the year isn't important. Maybe it's the day and month.'

'Go on . . .' I said.

'Well, Bowie was born on 8 January. Do you know who else was born then?' Dad went on to list the other people who might have had alien origins thanks to their connection to 8 January.

There's William Hartnell – the first ever actor to play *Doctor Who*. Hired to play the Doctor presumably because he was such a convincing alien!

Also born on 8 January was the King of Rock and Roll, Elvis Presley. There's a story that on the day that Elvis was born, a mysterious blue light was spotted hovering over his house. And according to his hairdresser/spiritual advisor, Elvis would sometimes recall that when he was eight years old, he was telepathically visited by aliens who showed him a future vision of 'a man wearing a white suit singing to a crowd'. Elvis would one day become a global superstar wearing exactly this!

Deciding to look into this 8 January alien theory, I discovered someone else who spoke a lot about aliens – the famous scientist Professor Stephen Hawking. I'm sure you know who Stephen Hawking is, but in case you don't, he was a brilliant scientist who studied black holes and was famously confined to a wheelchair after being diagnosed with a disease called ALS. Doctors told him he had two years to live, but he proved them wrong by living for over another fifty. Professor Hawking's theories were brilliant, but his thoughts on aliens terrified me. He thought we should stop trying to make contact with them IMMEDIATELY.

WHY WOULD ALIENS COME TO SEE US?

Why would aliens travel millions of miles to visit us? That's the big question Stephen Hawking wondered about. It is one that has generated many interesting answers.

Maybe they're tourists! This is the idea of the late author Iain M. Banks, who wrote in one of his novels that it's possible they might just be coming to witness a very rare thing . . . a solar eclipse. This is when the Moon crosses in front of the Sun, covering it up entirely, so that daytime briefly becomes night-time. Solar eclipses are fascinating to scientists, as they are basically an **IMPOSSIBLE THING**. The Moon is roughly four hundred times smaller than the Sun and is also about four hundred times closer to Earth, which is an astonishing coincidence, as it means they appear as almost exactly the same size in the sky to us. Apparently, this is an incredibly rare thing, and so, wrote Banks, perhaps aliens would like to come and see it in person.

NOTE TO SELF: Maybe we could trick the aliens into revealing themselves by selling them T-shirts with 'My mum travelled halfway across the universe to see an eclipse and all I got was this lousy T-shirt'.

Perhaps aliens are visiting us simply to bounce through the universe. This was an idea put forward by P.L. Travers, author of the *Mary Poppins* series, who seemed to believe in aliens. According to her writings, one day while out on a country walk, she spotted a patch of grass and flowers pressed into the ground. It was a very curious shape. These days, when people who believe in UFOs see grass pushed into the ground, they think it is possibly where a spacecraft has landed or where aliens have left messages in shapes and patterns for us to interpret (known as 'crop circles'). But Travers had a different idea. She believed that the shape was a giant footprint, left by an enormous alien from Uranus, who was using our planet as a stepping stone as it hopped its way through the universe. It's a shame she never wrote a book about this. I would have loved to read *Mary Poppins and the Big Foot from Uranus*.

Or is it possible they're coming simply to make us some pancakes? This was a question that plumber and part-time chicken farmer Joe Simonton found himself asking back in 1961, when he claimed that three aliens had landed their ship in his back yard in Wisconsin, USA. According to Simonton, they asked him for water, then cooked him some pancakes as a thank you before flying off. Interestingly, rather than brushing this story off, government officials took two of the pancakes away for testing. The results confirmed that they were, in fact, pancakes.

Hopefully the reason aliens would travel the universe to visit us is not the reason Professor Stephen Hawking believed it to be – which is to come and steal our resources. Worryingly, many scientists agree with Hawking, who warned us that by broadcasting our location and sending out messages into space, we might be attracting the attention of war-like aliens who want to take over our planet. Fortunately, so far none have come.

WHAT SHOULD WE SAY WHEN THE ALIENS ARRIVE?

Many people have debated how we should communicate with aliens when they arrive on Earth. Do we speak in a human language, do we play them music, do we use dance moves? There are thousands of ideas. One interesting idea that Professor Laurence Eaves from the University of Nottingham came up with is that we say nothing and just show them the number 137.

The reason for this is that 137 is one of the most mysterious numbers yet discovered by scientists. It's a number that keeps popping up in research and scientists just can't work out why. It's become such a curious number to science that many physicists believe it might explain some of the biggest mysteries of the universe. A universe that, incidentally, many scientists estimate to be around 13.7 billion years old.

It's a number that has obsessed great minds, like the Nobel Prize-winning physicist Wolfgang Pauli, who spent his life trying to understand what the number could mean. He was determined to crack the answer before he died. Unfortunately, death came for him much earlier than anyone would have hoped. One day Pauli suddenly became very ill and was quickly rushed to a hospital in Zurich, where he would die just a few days later. It didn't escape his attention, however, that the hospital room he would pass away in – randomly assigned to him – was room 137.

Professor Eaves believes that if we show the aliens the number 137 upon their arrival, they will know we are highly intelligent creatures and will not harm us as a result. Maybe they'll even make us some pancakes.

ALIENS ON VACAY!

WHAT IF WE ARE THE ALIENS?

One group of people also working on what to say to the aliens is called SETI (which stands for the Search for Extra-Terrestrial Intelligence), who for over 40 years now have been pointing radio telescopes at the skies, hoping to capture a message that has been beamed into space by an alien species. SETI even have someone on their staff who has been given the job of speaking to the aliens when they first land. SETI was created by a group of scientists, the leader of whom is one of my heroes, Frank Drake.

Drake explained the importance of listening out for radio signals from space roughly like this: Right now, as you sit reading this sentence, an alien message, sent by a civilisation millions of light years away, just passed through your head. At other times they have skimmed your elbows or brushed your toes, and you didn't even notice. At least, it's possible this has happened. What a thought! The answer to the question **'IS THERE LIFE IN THE UNIVERSE?'** just casually brushed against your right knee, before continuing through the centre of the Earth, out the other side and back into the inky void of our universe. But you'll never know. It's gone now. This could be happening all the time, but as of yet, no one's head has managed to catch the message being sent. And that's why we need as many radio telescopes trained at the skies as possible to catch them.

Drake spent his life coming up with amazing ways of communicating with aliens. He created the famous Drake equation, which was a calculation estimating how many aliens might live in our galaxy, and he even helped put together a music album full of songs and sent it into space, where it continues to travel out into the cosmos. But despite all his ideas, he never got a hello back from one.

Perhaps the alien Drake was looking for was staring right at his face the whole time. Literally. Maybe all he had to do was to look in a mirror. Because a lot of scientists think we humans might have come from outer space. This theory is called 'panspermia', and it proposes that life did not naturally begin on Earth, but rather it fell to Earth on a meteorite that carried alien life from a distant planet.

While this sounds a bit weird, a lot of scientists think this might have been how life began on our planet. Francis Crick, who co-discovered the structure of DNA (DNA is the information inside our bodies that helps make people who they are), thought not only that we could have arrived from space, but that an ancient civilisation might have purposefully sent a flask full of 'life' into the universe in the hope that it would eventually land on a planet and create beings.

Another science writer, Arthur C. Clarke, thought it wasn't impossible that a passing spaceship may have used our universe as a toilet and dropped their waste out of the ship. Then, because poo has living bacteria in it, life formed on our planet.

So, could we have come from the stars ourselves or were we born from an ancient extra-terrestrial civilisation's poo? We keep looking around to find aliens, but there's a big chance that we are them! We are the aliens. What a thought . . . and it's one that I think could really be true. What do you think?

This time it was me calling up my dad.

'Hi, Dan. What's up?' he said.

'Hey, Dad. I just wanted to call to apologise.'

'Oh yeah, what about?'

'It's just, I think you're right. Maybe David Bowie was an alien after all.'

CHAPTER 4
ARE TIME TRAVELLERS BAD PARTY GUESTS?

Aliens, Yetis and dead Tibetan nans aren't the only impossible people said to be walking among us. Many believe that we are crawling with time travellers too.

I once attempted to catch some myself. I did this by using a method that all Impossible Investigators must deploy at some point in their life. I threw a party exclusively for time travellers! I dressed the living room up with balloons and decorations, bought drinks and cake, and even made some very classy-looking invitations.

DEAR TIME TRAVELLERS OF THE FUTURE

THE SCHREIBERS WARMLY WELCOME YOU TO

A PARTY IN THE PAST!

WHEN: 18TH JULY 2024

TIME: 3-5 P.M.

LOCATION: YOU KNOW WHERE

FOOD AND DRINK WILL BE PROVIDED

SNEAKILY TELLING YOUR GREAT-GRANDPA THE WINNING LOTTO NUMBERS FOR NEXT WEEK'S DRAW IS A BIG NO-NO!

VISITS TO THE TOILET ARE STRICTLY FORBIDDEN!

Anyway, it was a disaster. Nobody came.

It was almost as bad as the time I threw a Past Life Party, where the idea was to come as somebody you were in a previous life. (This was in honour of my oldest son, Wilf, who had a very spooky experience one morning when he suddenly revealed that he could remember a life before this one. But that's a story for another book.)

I was excited for my Past Life Party. I was thinking it would be a clever way to guarantee a room full of historical-celebrity guests – everyone from Cleopatra to Elvis Presley would be there. Instead, it was only people like my friend Eric, who just came as himself. When I complained that he hadn't made any effort, he tried to pretend he had come as someone else: 'Uh, wait, I have come as someone. I'm astronaut Buzz Aldrin.'

'You can't come as Buzz Aldrin, Eric. He isn't even dead.'

'I mean I've come as a pig farmer from China in the, uhhh, Ming Dynasty.'

'Oh, yeah?' I said suspiciously. 'What's your name?'

'Uh, Eric,' he replied.

'There was an ancient Chinese farmer called Eric?'

'Uh, yeah,' he replied.

I wasn't buying any of it. Still, at least he came. Whereas at the Time Traveller Party, it was just me, my wife, Fenella, and my kids, Wilf, Ted and Kit, sitting around, bored and waiting.

I'm not the first to throw a Time Traveller Party. It has been a growing tradition among scientists. On 7 May 2005, students at the Massachusetts Institute of Technology (MIT), in the USA, threw a Time Traveller Convention. Co-ordinates were given so that any time traveller who wished to arrive would have a very specific landing pad to do so.

For any actual time travellers reading this book, the convention was held at 22.45 EDT in the East Campus Courtyard and Walker Memorial at MIT (42.360007 degrees north latitude, -71.087870 degrees west longitude).

Another Time Traveller Party was thrown by one of the greatest physicists of the modern world, whom you briefly met in the last chapter, Professor Stephen Hawking. As well as being a very serious scientist, he also had a silly side. He would often use his wheelchair to run over the toes of people who were annoying him and pretend it was an accident. He also threw cocktail parties for time travellers.

HOW TO THROW A PARTY FOR TIME TRAVELLERS

For those interested in following in my footsteps, here is an easy step-by-step guide for when you eventually get round to throwing your own party:

1. Write the invitations

2. Throw the party

3. Send out the invitations

Number 3 is the most important step. Don't send the invitations out before the party, because someone might see it and try to pretend to be a time traveller, just so they can come to your house and eat all your cakes and Monster Munch. I'm looking at you, Eric!

The information you put on the invitation is essential too. For example, time travellers absolutely must not share what they know about the future – like passing on the result of a football match to a younger version of themselves, or a relative, so they can place a bet on the match and make a fortune.

According to some people who believe in **IMPOSSIBLE THINGS**, there are actually companies around the world who are already taking action to prevent this from happening. In fact, there is a rumour that the National Lottery employs people whose job is to specifically stop time travellers coming back from the future to share the winning numbers with their friends and family! I personally don't think this exists, because if there really was some sort of Time Travellers Prevention Agency, I reckon people like my friend Buttons – who, as I explained earlier, often sits at home trying to channel the winning lottery numbers to his past self in the hope he'll win a week ago – would already have been arrested.

HOW TO INVENT TIME TRAVEL

There are so many things you could alter if you were to become a time traveller. Including inventing time travel itself! In fact, if you wanted to do that, it would be easy. All you'd need to do is travel to the year 1895 and make sure you popularise the idea of time travel before the science-fiction author H.G. Wells does it with his book *The Time Machine*.

Amazingly, Wells's book was the first to suggest a time-travelling device. Before that, anything to do with time travel involved people falling asleep and waking up in the future, or bumping their head and waking up in the past, or riding a magical hippogriff to get there. But the idea of travelling in a machine, one that specifically messes with the fabric of the universe to send you back in time like the TARDIS in *Doctor Who*, first appeared in Wells's novel.

So, if you want to become the inventor of the concept of time travel, all you need to do is travel back to a little over a century ago and pip H.G. Wells to the post. Unfortunately, in order to do that, you need a time machine – and we don't have one of those yet. But I'm definitely prepared for when we do finally get one. I've already been making a list of interesting places to visit (and you should too!).

EXTRACT FROM THE YOGIBOGEYBOOK #4

TIME-TRAVEL DESTINATIONS I WANT TO GO TO

1. THE DEATH OF CHEF JUAN RUIZ

There once was a chef called Juan Ruiz who met an impossible end. He was killed by flying spaghetti! According to the story, Chef Juan Ruiz was stabbed in the chest when uncooked strands of spaghetti were lifted into the air as 150 mph winds swept through his restaurant in Mexico City and stabbed him. This surely is impossible. I need to time travel back there to see if it is true. And then, if it is, stay over the next night to confirm whether it's true or not that they then took spaghetti bolognese off the menu as a mark of respect.

2. THE EXPLODING CHURCH

This trip would be to witness one of the most bizarre coincidences of all time (more of these later). It concerns a woman called Marilyn Paul and her mum, who were both part of the same choir. Every Wednesday they would head to the West Side Baptist Church in Beatrice, Nebraska, to join a group of thirteen others at 7.20 p.m. for an hour-long choir practice. But one day, on the evening of 1 March 1950, just 5 minutes after the practice was due to begin, the church suddenly EXPLODED. It was a huge explosion. So great, in fact, that the blast caused the whole building to collapse and even smashed the windows of nearby homes. Marilyn and her mum were usually on time for practice, but as luck would have it, Marilyn had gone for a quick nap and overslept. It took her mum so long to wake her that they ended up running late and, as a result, escaped certain death.

Here's the strange thing, though: they weren't the only ones who were running late that day. The Reverend, who was supposed to be there with his wife and daughter, was held up because his daughter stained her dress and had to change before they left. Others were late because they were listening to the end of radio shows, or the car wouldn't start, or they were trying to solve a hard geometry problem. Even Joyce Black, who lived literally across the road, didn't make it on time because she was just feeling lazy. Somehow, on this day, when fifteen people should have been singing inside the church as it exploded, every single one of them found themselves running late. It's impossible: all of them survived.

3. CHINA, MING DYNASTY
This is a quick trip, just to make sure there wasn't actually a farmer there called Eric.

4. THE SINKING OF THE TITANIC
On 15 April 1912, a ship called the *Titanic* sank after hitting an iceberg while on a journey from Southampton to New York City, killing over a thousand people. However, some say that this isn't quite right. According to one very odd theory the real reason it actually sank is not because of the iceberg, but because so many time travellers visited at the same time to see it hit the iceberg that the weight of them all pushed the ship beneath the water's surface.

NOTE TO SELF: Leave before you also sink with the other time travellers.

5. STEPHEN HAWKING'S TIME TRAVEL PARTY

And lastly, I would head to Cambridge University on 28 June 2009, where Stephen Hawking is hosting his party, and tell him that it worked! We cracked time travel. I'd eat as many cocktail sausages as possible, then quickly get out of there before Professor Hawking gets annoyed with me and tries to run over my toes.

HAS ANYONE EVER ACTUALLY MET A TIME TRAVELLER?

Stephen Hawking isn't the only physicist who has thought seriously about time travellers. Over at Oxford, one scientist potentially had an encounter with some. His name is David Deutsch. One day David got a call from his friend Ken. Ken had a problem: he had recently met someone claiming to be a time traveller but had no way of knowing if this man was telling the truth or not, so he asked if he could introduce him to David. Surely the clever scientist would be able to snoop out a fraud. Ken eventually arrived at David's door with a man called Falco, who told David he was from a place called Damanhur. They spent some time together, and when Falco left, Ken asked David if he thought Falco was telling the truth. David looked at Ken and said the chances that Falco was telling the truth were 50/50.

Usually when you hear a story like this, the time traveller disappears, never to be heard from again. But that's not the case for Falco . . .

THE ITALIAN TIME TRAVELLERS

Up in the hilltops of northern Italy is a small community called Damanhur. It was founded in 1975 by a man called Oberto Airaudi, also known as Falco, who wanted to build a secret temple inside the mountain so that he and his fellow Damanhurians could use it to save the planet. Now, usually when people build something, like a house or a temple, they have the idea first and then they build it. But we're dealing with time travel here, so in this case Falco built the temple first and then had the idea for it 600 years later.

Now, let's pause for a second to get our heads around this, because in order to understand the history of Damanhur, we need to travel to the future, all the way to the twenty-seventh century.

The story roughly goes like this: sometime, around the year 2600 CE, a group of leaders from various alien civilisations around the universe gathered together for their weekly Friday catchup. They were having a jolly time telling anecdotes, solving important issues and generally having some interesting chats, when someone (or some*thing* – I don't want to presume) eventually brought up the sad subject of the planet Earth. Oh, what a shame, they said, it used to be such a wonderful place, run by the humans living on it. However, ever since they were invaded by a hostile alien species, Earth had been all but destroyed and was now run by horrible extra-terrestrials who forced all of humankind to become their prisoners. At the end of the meeting one of the aliens was very sad. It didn't like what had happened to Earth, and decided to take pity on the human species by doing something about it. And so, it resolved to pre-incarnate itself (which is basically the opposite of reincarnate – it sent itself back in time, so it could be born again in the body of a human child).

The alien travelled back in time to the twentieth century and was born on Earth as a human baby named Oberto Airaudi. This boy, who would later rename himself Falco, would then dedicate his life to saving mankind by creating a community of time travellers to help stop the impending alien invasion.

Astonishingly, Falco managed to convince a whole group of people about his alien origins, and they all then spent 23 years helping him dig into a mountain to build a temple of wonder. It's as big as St Paul's Cathedral in London, if you've ever been there or seen a picture, and it has nine chambers, secret stairways, a labyrinth and a 'fully functioning time machine'!

Eventually, the Italian government found out about the community and visited it with the intention of shutting it down. But when they got there they were amazed at what Falco and his followers had built, and declared it the 'eighth wonder of the world'. It was given a Guinness World Records title for the 'World's Largest Underground Temple' too. To this day, residents of the commune are said to continue to use the temple to travel back in time to Atlantis, which apparently has great shops.

A TRIP BACK IN TIME

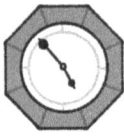

You can actually visit Damanhur if you want, by the way. It really does exist, and they rent out rooms there for visitors. It currently has a 4.5 rating on TripAdvisor. Though if you mention time travel, they'll almost certainly deny it happens, as they are probably trying to protect their work and secrets.

For those in the UK who can't quite make it to a northern Italian mountain, there is somewhere a bit more local where you can attempt to travel back in time, and that's in Liverpool.

I recently read about a bizarre place called Bold Street, where it has been reported that people who walk along it have sometimes momentarily found themselves slipping back into the 1950s and 60s. I once went to Liverpool to see it, but unfortunately got sidetracked when the pub I was having lunch in turned out to be haunted, and by the time I'd investigated that, I had – ironically – run out of time. (But that is a story for another book.)

Many people have reported strange experiences while walking on Bold Street. The first was in 1996, when a policeman called Frank was shopping with his wife, Carol. According to the story, Carol went off to buy a book from a shop called Dillons, and Frank went to find her about 20 minutes later. While on his way, Frank was nearly hit by a car. Shocked, Frank looked at the car and noticed that it didn't look like any other car he'd seen before – it was something out of the 1950s. *Strange*, thought Frank. As he reached the bookshop, things continued to get weird. Instead of the latest books in the window, there were shoes and handbags, and the sign above the door read 'Cripps'. When Frank walked into the shop, he noticed everyone was wearing 1950s clothing. What on earth was going on? Suddenly everything morphed back into the present day. What had happened? Was he hallucinating? He must have been. Later, Frank decided to look into the location of this Dillons, and there, in the historical records, was a description of a ladies' outfitters and dressmakers . . . called Cripps.

This phenomenon has come to be known as the 'Bold Street timeslip'. Multiple people have claimed it has happened to them too, and you don't even need a time machine to get there.

DO NOT POO IN THE PAST!

Well, it finally hit 6 p.m., and no time travellers had shown up to my party. We wrapped the cakes up, put them in the fridge, popped a bunch of the balloons, and I took down the sign on the bathroom door that read, 'Oy! Stay out of here, future person!'

That's the last thing you'll notice on the invitation to my Time Traveller Party – guests cannot go to the loo. I learned this from reading about the Damanhurians, who are trained to not poo when they travel to another bit of history. This is incredibly important. You see, there may be bacteria in your faeces from modern diseases that were not around in the past. This can be very dangerous. If someone from our time travelled back to, say, the time of the cavemen, a single trip to the toilet could release a plague and wipe out all of humanity. So remember, if you wipe your bum in the past, it won't be the only thing you're wiping away.

NUMBER TWOS HAVE CONSEQUENSES

Once the toilet sign was down, I got my two older boys, Wilf and Ted, to join me in putting on our coats, scarves and shoes. Waving goodbye to Fenella and Kit, we went to do something very important. The last step to ensure a successful Time Traveller Party.

'We'll be back soon, Mummy,' yelled Ted. 'We're just off to the postbox to send out some invitations to the future.'

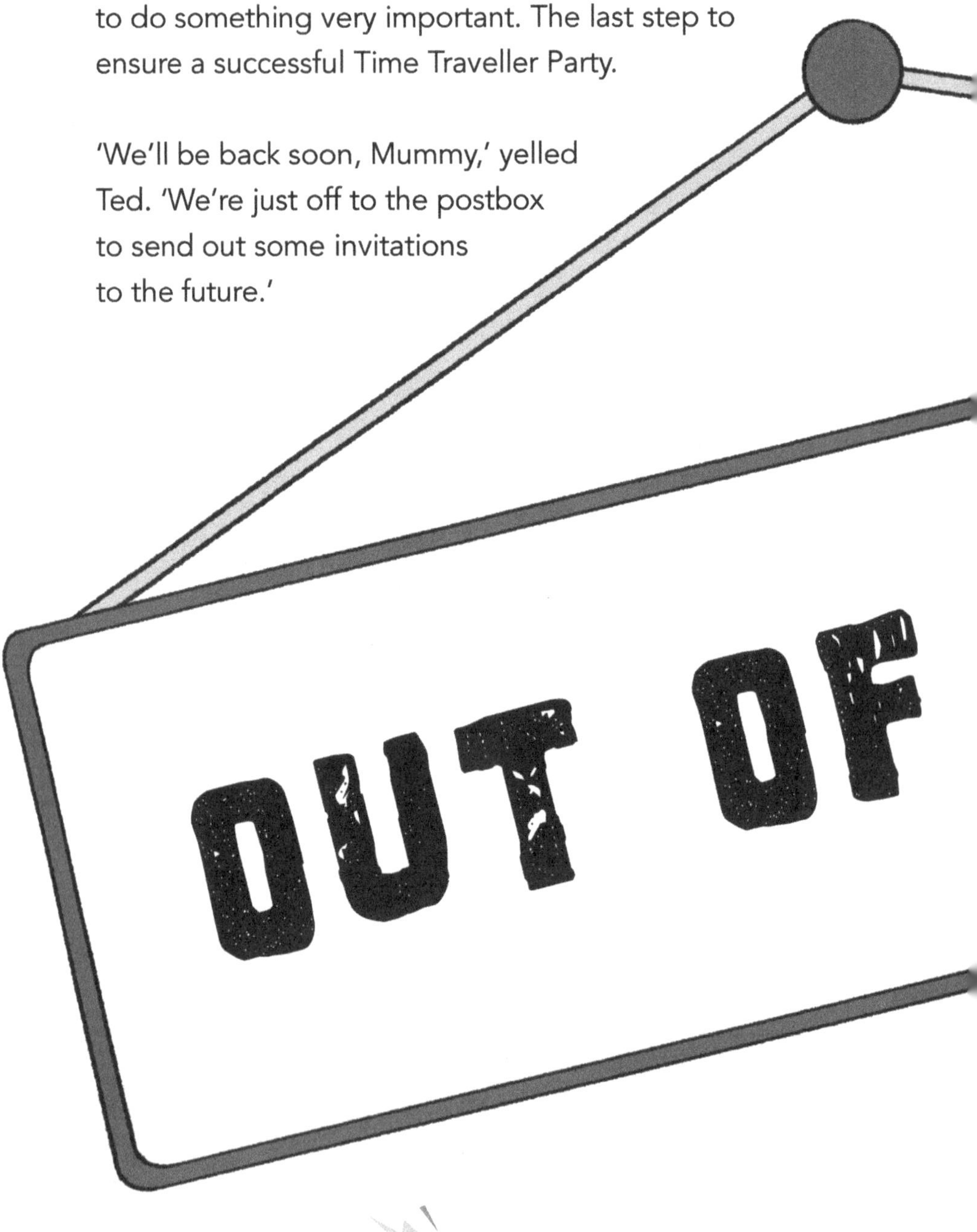

CHAPTER 5

DO I NEED GLASSES FOR THE EYES IN THE BACK OF MY HEAD?

In 1984, America's Central Intelligence Agency, also known as the CIA (where all their international spies work), attempted something impossible. On 22 May they tried to send one of their spies to the planet Mars, a million years in the past!

There was no rocket ship involved. No bending the universe to plop this spy into the past. Instead, a spy called Joseph McMoneagle was brought into a room and told that on the table was an envelope with instructions of a place they wanted him to visit written inside. He wasn't told where this was, or what time in history it was. All he had were some directions: '40.89 degrees north; 9.55 degrees west'. Joseph closed his eyes, pictured what was in the envelope and then transported his mind to the location described. He saw yellow landscapes, shadowy figures, pyramid-like objects and caves.

All this was recorded and filed in a document called 'Mars Exploration'. What the CIA did with this information, we don't know. What we do know is that this experiment was not an isolated one, and that for over 20 years the Agency spent more than $20 million recruiting and training agents to spy on their enemies and gain secret information using this method.
The CIA were trying to invent
a new kind of soldier:
the psychic spy!

A psychic spy is someone who should have the ability to travel to a place using just their mind. In theory it's a great idea. Imagine getting somewhere without having to move. This means psychic spies would be able to sit in class at school every day, without ever needing to actually get out of bed.

I became interested in the idea of psychic spies when I made the shocking discovery that one of my friends was one. A few months after triumphantly securing the world's oldest ghost a Guinness World Records title, I met up with the editor-in-chief Craig Glenday so I could talk to him about some of the **IMPOSSIBLE THINGS** he had learned while travelling the world. 'Hmmm . . . I'm not sure I'm all that weird,' he said in his thick Scottish accent. Then he dropped the bombshell: 'Oh . . . there was the time I trained to be a psychic spy.'

'What???' I stared at Craig in disbelief.

'Yeah, I'm technically a psychic spy. I have no idea if I can really do it, but I do have a certificate to prove I'm one,' he replied.

Craig explained that before he worked for Guinness World Records he was once the editor of a magazine called *The X Factor*, which isn't anything to do with the TV show, but was instead an exciting magazine that investigated all the **IMPOSSIBLE THINGS** that humans claimed they could do. One of those things was being psychic.

'Do you think you could read my mind?' I asked Craig.

'Dunno. I'll give it a go,' he replied.

Craig had trained with someone who claimed to be a former CIA operative called Tim. His training session happened somewhere in a building on the seafront in Brighton, and Tim the Spy had Craig, and all the other people on the course, attempt to train their minds to leave their body and appear in another location. The location Tim picked was Loch Ness, and he wanted his students to spy on the monster. (Little did Tim know that Nessie, if it exists at all, might have telepathic powers and would presumably block their attempts.)

'OK,' said Craig, 'before we begin, I'm going to need you to grab a piece of paper and a pen. Then, draw something on the paper, but don't show it to me and don't say anything. Something simple. Then describe your picture to yourself in your head, not out loud. I will read your mind and draw the exact same image on my piece of paper.'

While Craig was giving me my instructions, I took out my **YOGIBOGEYBOOK** and started to draw a picture, being careful to keep it hidden from Craig. I had decided on a UFO with a big tractor beam coming down. Here's the picture I drew.

Once I was done, I let Craig know he could start looking into my mind. I wondered if I would feel anything as he did his rummaging. Would I feel like someone was making a mess of the filing system in my brain as Craig popped in there to find the image I had just drawn?

MY DRAWING

WHAT IS MIND TREKKING?

Maybe this psychic thing was possible – our brains are pretty incredible objects. According to scientists they are the most complicated objects that we've found in the known universe. How amazing is that? So far, nothing out there, and that includes the brains of every other species on Earth, compares with that 3 pound lump sitting in your head.

For centuries people have claimed they can do some pretty incredible things with their brains: they can lift objects up using their mind (that's called telekinesis); they can read people's mind (that's called psychic reading, or telepathy); and some people believe they can even do things like know when someone standing behind them is staring at them.

THE SENSE OF BEING STARED AT

Have you ever wondered if your teacher has eyes in the back of their head? Well, according to one scientist, Rupert Sheldrake, they basically do. Rupert Sheldrake has been staring at people as they stare at other people for decades now. He believes that this is an extra sense, and he's not alone. Millions of people have experienced it. However, because there has yet to be any conclusive evidence that it is definitely happening, scientists remain sceptical about Sheldrake's ideas.

Regardless, according to Sheldrake, this 'sense' has influenced the world in many interesting ways. For example, Sheldrake was once told by a high-ranking officer that in the Second World War, when RAF fighter pilots had their enemy in sight, they were advised not to stare at that enemy pilot for too long before taking a shot, as the intensity of their gaze would alert the enemy to their position. According to Sheldrake, not only do we know when we are being stared at, but we know the direction from which we are being stared at.

Interestingly, many of the people you have met in this book believe they know when they're being stared at. Dr Irving Finkel, the curator from the British Museum who found the world's oldest ghost, believes in it; in fact, he often sits on London buses on his way home from work staring at the back of people's heads, trying to get them to turn around ('And they do!' says Irving). Then there's Steve Feltham, the Nessie hunter who believes he can achieve this too. I have definitely felt the sensation of it, though I can't be sure I was right every time I've felt it. Why not give it a go next time you're in a room full of people and someone has their back to you?

THE PROBLEM WITH TELEPATHY

It had been a while now since Craig started staring into my eyes. I hoped he wasn't able to see all my thoughts as he rooted around for my drawing. What if he came across a great idea for an invention I'd had, or managed to stumble on the exact co-ordinates for the location of a hidden treasure that I knew about and was keeping a secret from everybody (perhaps that's another story for another book). He could steal these things and claim them as his own!

This is something that has worried many people, like the American author Mark Twain, who wrote the books *The Adventures of Tom Sawyer* and *Adventures of Huckleberry Finn*. Twain believed we could communicate telepathically. So much so that he even thought up an invention for someone to try to build.

He called it the 'phrenophone!' It was meant to work in a similar way to a telephone, the main difference being that, instead of dialling a number, you could simply think the command, like, 'Connect me to the brain of Bhutan's royal Yeti hunter!', and it would.

While excited by this idea, Twain was also very worried about the illegal side of telepathy, and even went as far as accusing an equally famous author of stealing his idea.

In 1907, when a new story by the Irish playwright George Bernard Shaw was published, Twain noticed that it was incredibly similar to one that he had written 17 years before but had not published. According to Twain there was only one way Shaw could have got the idea: *He stole the story directly from my thoughts.*

Not that Twain himself was innocent of stealing ideas. He admitted that while he did have original ideas, he must also have been taking them from somewhere else. In fact, Twain thought that might be the reason why certain things are invented by two different people, on opposite sides of the world, at the exact same time.

This has happened. One incredible example of that involved the *Beano* comic character Dennis the Menace. You might know that as well as there being a British character called Dennis the Menace, there is an American Dennis the Menace, who also wears a striped T-shirt, is also accompanied by a dog and also likes to cause mischief with a slingshot. What you might not know is that these two characters first appeared on the **EXACT SAME DAY**. And neither of the cartoonists had copied each other. They both came up with the idea independent of each other. An amazing coincidence? Or did the impossible happen and each cartoonist's brain picked up the same idea from the other somehow?

TIN FOIL PROTECTION AGENCY

So if our brains are leaking thoughts, what can we do about it? Well, some people became so concerned about it that they actually invented a device to stop it from happening: a tin foil hat! For many years now some people have been wearing these hats with the belief that the tin would scramble any attempt to steal their thoughts or read their minds.

The truth is there is no evidence to show that we can steal people's thoughts. So tin foil hats are useless. Worse still, a few years ago, some MIT students discovered that even if wearing a tin foil hat did work, it would have the opposite effect from what was intended. It actually **AMPLIFIES** the signal, making it easier to steal your thoughts. So don't wear a tin foil hat if you want to keep your thoughts a secret.

WHAT HAS TELEPATHY EVER DONE FOR US?

So far, we have no proof that telepathy works, but that doesn't mean it hasn't helped to change the world. One important contribution came about in 1892 after a nineteen year old called Hans Berger fell off his horse during a military exercise and was nearly crushed to death by the wheel of an artillery cannon; however, as luck would have it, the horse pulling the cannon stopped just in time and he avoided death. Later that day, a telegram arrived for Hans. It was from his father, who was writing to say that earlier that day Hans's sister had experienced a sudden and terrifying feeling that her brother was in trouble and insisted he write to Hans to make sure he was OK. How could she have possibly known that he had been in danger?

Most would chalk this up as a coincidence, but Hans became convinced that the only way she could have known was via telepathy. Hans decided to see if he could find the bit of the brain that was transmitting these telepathic thoughts. Thirty years later, Hans invented a machine that could scan brains. It is called an electroencephalography machine, or an EEG for short. And while it failed to prove that telepathy exists, even a hundred years later it is still one of the most important medical inventions we have, scanning the brains of patients to diagnose what is going wrong.

PSYCHIC INTUITION

'So how are you actually doing this?' I asked Craig, who was still staring into my eyes.

'I just get a feeling, I suppose,' he said. 'It's like a gut feeling, and you have to trust your gut.'

I know that feeling. That's what Hans Berger's sister had when he fell off the horse. It's what my mum says every time anyone ever calls her: 'I knew you were going to call, I was just thinking of you this morning.' It's a very strong feeling about something.

Psychic intuition is something that many people think they have, and as a result it has been used many times on TV police shows and in detective books, so much so that people have started to believe it's an actual job you can get, called a profiler. That job doesn't exist. However, so many people think that it does that organisations like the American Federal Bureau of Investigation (FBI) have even had to release this statement:

> *The FBI does not have a job called 'profiler'. Despite some popular depictions, these FBI special agents do not get 'vibes' or experience 'psychic flashes' while walking around fresh crime scenes.*

While agencies and scientists deny this is an actual ability, psychic intuition has had some pretty curious moments. A notable example being the time that a British movie script writer experienced a psychic feeling, decided to follow her intuition and ended up discovering the missing bones of one of England's most famous kings …

A STRANGE ENCOUNTER WITH RICHARD III

The story I'm about to tell you is a strange tale.

Richard III was the King of England from 1483 until his death in 1485. You know him: he was accused of killing his two nephews in a tower; he had a curved spine; Shakespeare wrote a play about him. Well, despite being one of our most famous kings, for many hundreds of years we lost him. No one could remember where he was buried, and there were many years of speculation about where he may have been buried.

Then, one day in 2004, a screenwriter called Philippa Langley was on a research trip gathering information for a movie she was trying to write about Richard III, when suddenly an odd feeling came over her while standing inside a car park in Leicester. She was struck by the sudden revelation that right below her feet was the long-lost body of the very man she was researching.

Returning home, Philippa continued work on her script, but she couldn't shake off the idea that the king was there, buried under the tarmac. Over the next 12 months she would explain it to her friends and family, who encouraged her not to dispel the feeling. What if she was right? And so Langley decided to return to the car park, curious to see if that same feeling would come to her again. It did, and this time there was an even greater sign that she needed to act on it. A literal sign. 'Slightly to my left, on the tarmac, there was something new – a white hand-painted letter R,' she wrote. Now, to anyone else, that 'R' painted on the floor is obviously a letter indicating a 'reserved' parking spot, but to Philippa, in that moment, it stood for Richard – as if the universe was literally spelling it out for her.

Over the next 6 years she attempted to fundraise the cash and obtain permissions for a team to dig down underneath the R. An archaeological team from the University of Leicester came onboard, and when digging finally commenced, it was on the very first day, and just a few metres from the R that they hit on bones! And not only were they human bones, but they were later confirmed to be King Richard III's bones. Philippa had done it! She had helped to find the lost king.

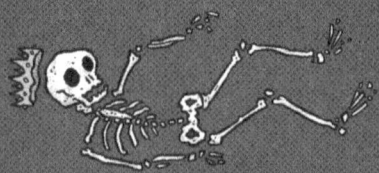

The king's body was eventually identified using the DNA from one of his descendants, a man called Michael Ibsen, who is a seventeenth-generation descendent of Richard III's sister, Anne of York.

The idea that King Richard was discovered by this psychic intuition is only one side to this extraordinary find; there is also the incredible work by the academic community, particularly the two leading academics on the dig. It's fair to say that they don't believe there was anything mystical about the king's discovery. However, I will point out that it is rather curious that two of the project leaders who went on to find his bones were called Turi **KING** and **RICHARD** Buckley.

There has been much bickering and mudslinging between Philippa Langley and the archaeologists in the years since the discovery, both believing they haven't been properly credited for their part in the discovery. And they're both right. But the truth is that they couldn't have done it without each other. A perfect example of the impossible and the scientific working together!

Of course, one person, who has been sitting in the background, unacknowledged in this strange tale, is the woman who accurately worked out where the king was buried long before anyone else did. Back in 1962, the same year that Philippa Langley was born, a request to dig up the very car park where Richard was found was sent in by an academic, but her request was denied. In 1975, she even published a paper so that others could see where the king would be found. Still, no one did anything about it. Sadly, she died in 2010, just 2 years before the king was found in the exact area she said he would be. But she shouldn't be forgotten, because she is the start of this bizarre story. It is a strange tale, or more accurately, it's A. Strange tale, because that woman who started it all was called Audrey Strange!

As for King Richard III, he was eventually reburied in Leicester Cathedral, in a casket made by his descendent, Michael Ibsen.

My hope is that one day this will lead to even more confusion. Imagine if through the passage of time the site of Richard III's grave is once again lost. And 500 years from now, another Philippa Langley comes along to find the lost king. Imagine those future archaeologists scratching their heads, trying to work out the mystery of how King Richard III was buried in a coffin built by his great-great-great-great-great-great-great-great-great-great-great-great-great-great-great-great nephew!

TELEKINESIS

Craig had now picked up his pen and was continuing to stare into my eyes. Without breaking eye contact he was drawing on his paper. Maybe he thought he had finally found the drawing of the UFO in my mind using his psychic intuition.

Psychic intuition and telepathy aren't the only two things people believe we can achieve with our minds. Perhaps the weirdest one of all is telekinesis, which is the idea of lifting and moving objects using only our brains.

At moments like these I can't help but once again think about my sister and that weird ghostly event in Tibet. Maybe it wasn't a ghost after all, but my sister achieving telekinesis. Is it possible that she lifted the glass up using her mind? This is also an **IMPOSSIBLE THING** that scientists don't believe in. Which is why it's so odd that perhaps one of the best claims for its existence happens to have been associated with one of the world's greatest scientists.

THE MAN WHO BROKE EVERYTHING

We already met Wolfgang Pauli briefly in chapter 3. He's the Nobel Prize-winning scientist who was obsessed with the number 137 (and who later died in the room with the same number). One of the odd mysteries that came to consume his life was the fact that every time he went near any electrical equipment, it would break. Fellow scientists dubbed it the 'Pauli effect'.

It happened so often that people started to log each occurrence, like the time Pauli was visiting the town of Princeton to do some research and a machine in the lab at the nearby Princeton University spontaneously combusted, resulting in a fire that burned for more than 6 hours. Or the time a measuring device at the University of Göttingen randomly broke. James Franck, the lab's director, jokingly enquired if Pauli was in town. He wasn't. Franck later wrote to Pauli to tell him about the incident, only to receive a letter back explaining that, actually, on the day of the explosion, Pauli had caught a train to Copenhagen and had to change trains in Göttingen, which meant he was in town on the day the machine broke!

As more and more examples of the Pauli effect continued to pile in, many scientists reportedly started getting nervous about his presence around their incredibly expensive equipment – Nobel Prize-winning physicist Otto Stern even banned Pauli from his lab!

Others saw it as funny – one group of scientists played a trick on Pauli to make him believe he was the cause of chaos by rigging a chandelier to fall from the ceiling as soon as he walked into the room. However, when he arrived, the mechanism built to drop the chandelier got stuck and the prank failed – further proving his effect.

While the term was a joke to many within the scientific community, Pauli certainly wasn't laughing, as he genuinely believed something telekinetic was going on. Whenever objects blew up around him, Pauli claimed to have felt an energy building up within him before the object broke.

POOR PAULI

Sadly, Pauli passed away before he, or we, could find out what was going on. Can we sense when we are being stared at? Are people stealing ideas from our minds? Can our minds access things from the future? We just don't know. So far no one has proven these things to be definitely true. Perhaps that's a job for you!

CRAIG FINISHES RUMMAGING

'Done,' said Craig. 'This obviously won't work. As I said, I have the certificate, but I'm not sure any of it is real.'

Still, I thought, *it'll be fun to see how close Craig gets to the image I have drawn.* Even if I knew there was no chance he was going to step into my mind and find the image of the UFO with tractor beams, it does seem like an interesting way to train your brain to think differently. Why not see if you and your friends could be psychic spies too? Just take it in turns to draw a picture and then try to read each other's minds to see what each other has drawn.

Craig and I both revealed our drawings at the same time and lay them down next to each other.

'NOOOOOOO WAAAAAAAAAYYYYY!!!!' we both yelled out in shock.

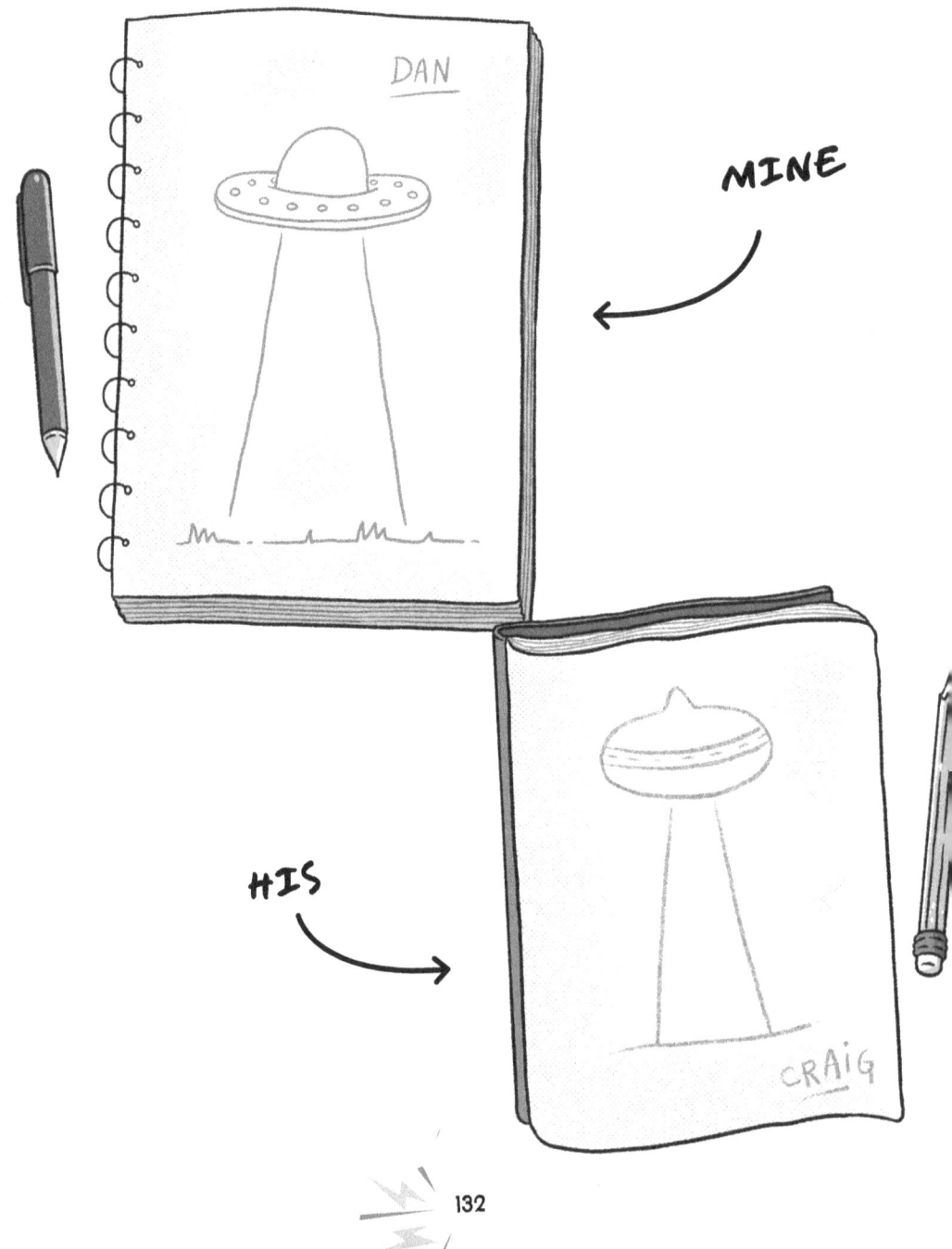

There they were, two drawings of a UFO, almost exactly the same, lying before us.

'Maybe I am a psychic spy!' said Craig. 'I wonder where I should send my mind next?'

'I know,' I replied. 'Next stop: Mars, in the year one million BCE!'

Chapter 6
Should We Be Learning to Speak Cat?

If you are planning on becoming a true investigator of the impossible, then one thing you're going to have to do is get comfortable with the fact that sometimes you are going to look a bit looney. In this specific case, by trying to start conversations with plants, trees and animals.

Wouldn't you love to chat to a dolphin and find out what is going on in the sea? Or update a beehive on the daily news? (More on this later.)

If you ever want to do this, don't worry, you won't be alone in your attempts. Some of the greatest minds in the world have looked bananas trying to communicate with things that don't talk back (like bananas).

Take Charles Darwin, for example. He is one of the greatest scientists ever to live – he's the man behind the theory of evolution (the idea that all living things share a common ancestor). Even he wasn't above looking a bit crackers. In December 1878, Darwin walked into his garden with his son Francis, and together they played a bassoon at his mimosa plants to see if they could hear it. Darwin hoped that the music would excite them into a 'dance'. Some musical notes were played and Darwin was amazed to see some plants move. Had he done it? Had Charles Darwin communicated with plants? It turned out: no. When he tried to repeat the experiment using a different method, nothing happened. In fact, he called it his 'fool's experiment'. So, despite all that he achieved, Darwin went to his grave having never managed to influence the plant world with sound.

DCI BAXTER REPORTING FOR DUTY

Just because it didn't work for Darwin, doesn't mean we shouldn't continue trying. For the last few weeks I have been attempting to chat to my houseplant, which I've named Baxter; it sits next to me in my office, watching me as I work. As I don't own a bassoon, I've instead taken to trying to communicate with it by constantly telling it impossible facts. For example: 'Baxter, did you know that it has been estimated that a human fart travels at more than twice the speed a sloth can walk.' But so far Baxter has not responded to me.

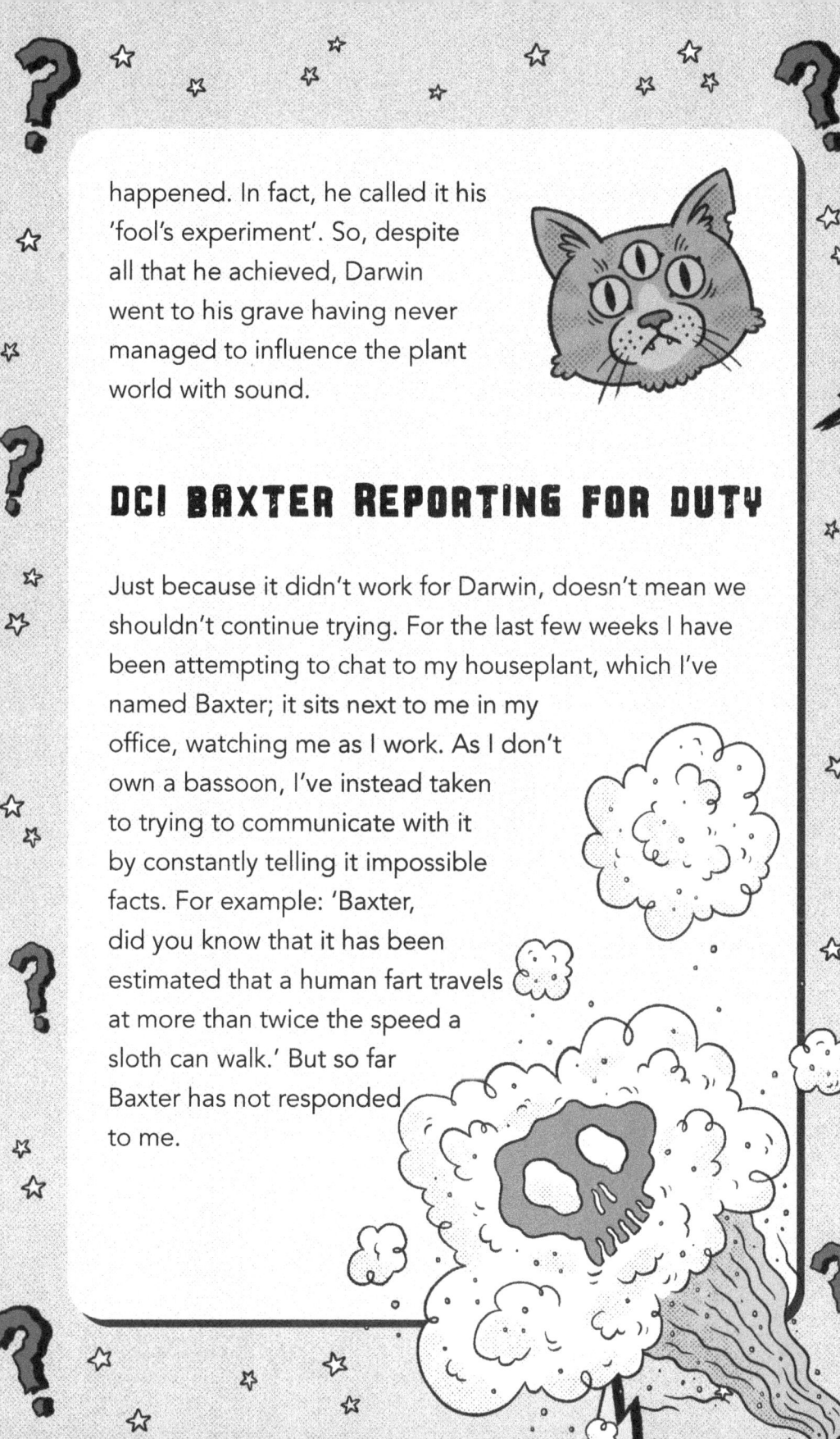

I named the plant Baxter after a man called Cleve Backster, who claimed to be the first person to achieve what Darwin failed to do: get a reaction from the plant world. Cleve was a former CIA employee whose job it was to use lie detectors on criminals. One night Cleve thought for fun he would try out his lie detector on his office plant. He hooked the plant up and, after running a few tests, noticed that the lie-detecting machine started to give readings, as if the plant were a human. *Impossible!* thought Cleve. So he tried another test to see if the plant was really giving genuine reactions to the lie detector. When interrogating a criminal, one way to get a reaction out of them for a lie detector machine is to scare them. And so Cleve decided to scare the plant by threatening to set it on fire. And that's when things got weird, according to Backster. Immediately after thinking about setting the plant on fire, the lie detector registered a huge spike, as if the plant had read Cleve's mind and had become terrified by the threat. *Whoa,* thought Cleve. *Did I just become the first person in history to communicate with a plant?*

Cleve continued to experiment with his plants and had a big breakthrough when he tested to see if they could spot a criminal in a police line-up. In this experiment, Cleve placed two office plants in a room, and he had someone go into that room and rip one of the plants out of the pot and stamp on it. He then had six people walk into the room, including the plant destroyer, to see if the remaining plant would show any reaction on the lie detector machine when the killer walked back in. **AND IT DID!** According to Cleve, the plant picked out the right person!

This is incredible, thought Cleve. *Imagine a world where criminals could be arrested based on the testimony of a plant that witnessed a crime happen when no humans were around to see it.* The police should be recruiting them at once! And it wasn't only police work that they could be used for: plants could be recruited by the army and could spy on the enemy who were walking past them in the field; they could even become astronauts and be sent into deep space, reporting back to us from millions of miles away.

Unfortunately, Cleve's research is yet to be proven correct so we don't have a special police force made up of houseplants. One day, maybe!

It isn't just plants we've attempted to talk to, of course. There's the animal kingdom too.

WHAT IS A PARROT'S FAVOURITE COLOUR?

Now, this book is full of weird questions, but perhaps none of them are weirder than this one: 'What colour?'

The reason it is so weird is because, according to scientist Dr Irene Pepperberg, a parrot called Alex asked it.

Now, we know parrots can mimic words. In fact, it has made for some weird news reports over the years.

There's the parrot who belonged to Andrew Jackson, the seventh president of the United States, named Polly. Jackson loved Polly; so much so that Polly was even allowed to attend the president's funeral. Jackson taught Polly to say a lot of words - unfortunately, some of them were rude, so Polly had to be removed from the funeral because she wouldn't stop swearing.

Another parrot, called Me-Tu, had to be removed from a football match between Hatfield Town and Hertford Heath when it started mimicking the referee's whistle, causing confusion for the players.

There's the heavy metal band called Hatebeak, whose lead singer is a grey parrot called Waldo. Waldo has sung all the songs on all their albums.

> And then there's Nigel, a parrot who spoke with a British accent. One day Nigel mysteriously went missing, though thanks to a microchip he was found 4 years later. Nigel clearly had quite the adventure, because when he returned, his owners found that he could speak Spanish and kept humming the opening bars of the theme tune from a very old cowboy movie called *The Good, the Bad and the Ugly*.

There are many more examples of talking parrots. But what makes Alex the parrot's speech so important is that it might just be the first existential question ever to be asked by a non-human! 'What colour?' All these other parrots were just repeating things they had been told. But Alex actually asked a question about itself!

The answer was grey. And Alex learned the word after hearing it just six times. As far as we know, no other species on our planet asks questions like this. It's called self-awareness. When you are suddenly aware of yourself as an individual. Scientists are generally dubious that Alex achieved this milestone, as there isn't enough research and evidence to back up the claim, but if true, then Alex became self-aware when he asked that question!

Humans are very self-aware. That's why we love talking so much! A quick flick through my **YOGIBOGEYBOOK** reveals a great growing list titled 'ATTEMPTS TO CHAT TO ANIMALS'.

People try to talk to bees . . .

There is a tradition for beekeepers to tell their bees when big news has happened. Like when there's a birth or a wedding or a death. It is a very old tradition, but it continues to this day. When Queen Elizabeth II died, her bees were informed by the head beekeeper, who knocked on each of the hives before saying, 'The mistress is dead, but don't you go. Your master will be a good master to you.' The idea is that you need to do this, otherwise the bees will become angry and abandon the hives.

People try to talk to monkeys . . .

Zookeepers communicate with monkeys all the time – sometimes even having to learn a different language to do so, like the staff at Port Lympne Safari Park in Kent, who took in some baboons from France. They quickly learned that the baboons didn't speak English, and they had to start speaking to them in French to let them know when lunch was ready.

People try to talk to dogs . . .

Just like monkeys, dogs can be trained to understand words like 'walkies' and 'din-dins', but I doubt very much you have ever met a dog that spoke English. However, one man was convinced he could teach his dog to do just that. Alexander Graham Bell, the inventor of the telephone, spent ages trying to get his dog to speak, and eventually managed to get him to growl, 'How are you, Grandmama?'

People try to talk to cats . . .

A friend of mine, Ed, who doesn't believe anything impossible happens, recently admitted a curious thing to me. He said that every time he is walking down a street on his own, he'll hear someone say, 'ED! ED!' out loud, and whenever he turns, there is never a human there, but there is always a cat.

'Ed,' I said. 'Are you telling me you think cats are talking to you in English?'

'No, of course not,' he replied. 'I'm just saying that cats seem to be calling out my name when no one else is around, and even though I don't believe it, it's definitely happening.' Ah, the great puzzle of the unbeliever to whom the unbelievable happens.

It would be great if cats could talk to us, as there is a theory that they might hold the key to one of the mysteries of our planet: when an earthquake is going to hit. We humans have spent centuries trying to accurately predict earthquakes, but we just can't seem to do it.

But, according to one Californian geologist named Jim Berkland, cats can. Berkland claimed to have successfully predicated two earthquakes by tracking the number of ads for missing cats in newspapers. Berkland believed that cats knew when an earthquake was coming and would run away. In fact, he noticed a 400% increase in missing cat ads in the lead up to an earthquake. Many believed he was on to something with this theory, and even raised the idea of setting up an earthquake hotline, where people could report their missing cats so that geologists would know when a quake was coming. Sadly, it was never realised. Though perhaps we can get my friend Ed to ask the cats directly next time they try to talk to him.

A FELINE WARNING

People try to talk to dolphins . . .

There once was a scientist called John Lilly, who tried to train dolphins to speak English so that they could tell the leaders of the world what the mammals living in the ocean thought. NASA was so convinced by his research that they funded his project, and the scientist started to plan a house that could be lived in by humans and dolphins. There would be rooms for dolphins, rooms for humans and then rooms for both dolphins and humans, like the dining room, where the dinner table would have water coming halfway up the table's legs, so that both dolphin and human could eat food in each other's company. He even worked on a flooded car design for the dolphins, so that they could transport themselves between locations.

The house was built, and for many months dolphins and humans did live together, sharing a dining room. However, the project came to an end before any real breakthroughs could be made. The dream of communicating with these ocean mammals continues today, and some scientists are even currently working on a dolphin-language dictionary.

Despite all our efforts so far, we haven't managed to talk to the plant world or the animal kingdom. But that hasn't stopped us from trying. As you've just read, we humans are constantly trying to have impossible conversations.

Perhaps one day we will work out how to speak to something non-human. And for that reason, I will continue to talk to my plant Baxter, and try to astonish it into communicating back. 'Hey, Baxter, did you know that Bigfoot, Texas in America is not named after the mysterious beast, but is instead named after a local ranger who just had really big feet?' Still nothing …

One glimmer of hope came in 2009 when the Royal Horticultural Society did a month-long study to see if tomato plants grow taller when being spoken to by a human. Though the experiment was more fun than scientific, it yielded a very interesting result. Ten people were selected and paired up with a different plant, for which they each recorded an audiobook of their choice. This was then played to the specific plant on a loop via a set of headphones placed around the plant pot. At the end of the experiment the plant that was found to have grown the most – by over half an inch – was the one listening to *On the Origin of Species*, which was being read to it by the great-great granddaughter of the author, Charles Darwin.

Though he'll never know it, over 120 years after his attempt to get a reaction from plants by playing the bassoon to them, Charles Darwin finally managed his goal! Only he didn't do it with music, but instead through his words.

CHAPTER 7
CAN IMAGINARY FRIENDS COME TO LIFE?

As you will have noticed from reading this book by now, a lot of what being an Impossible Investigator involves is travelling long distances to *not* see something. So far I have told you how I went to Loch Ness and didn't see Nessie; how I've stared through the window of a café in Yeovil Junction train station and didn't witness a levitating buffet; and how I threw a party and didn't meet any time travellers.

But now I want to tell you about perhaps the weirdest journey I've made to *not* see something. And that's the time I travelled to New York City to *not* see someone's imaginary friend.

New York is home to all sorts of weirdness, but to me there is no greater mystery than what might be going on inside the home of number 12 Gay Street. You see, it is believed that inside this house is a fictional character who somehow came to life.

IMPOSSIBLE? Well, the curious thing is this: it doesn't even appear to be a one-off. Many others have reported seeing people who shouldn't exist suddenly appear in front of them.

CAN FICTIONAL CHARACTERS BECOME REAL?

Many years ago, a comic book writer called Alan Moore was sitting on the upstairs floor of a London sandwich shop, chewing away on some food, when he noticed a man walking up the stairs. Alan was dumbfounded – he knew this man, but . . . no, there was just no way he could really be standing there in front of him. It was impossible! Maybe it was a lookalike? Maybe he was dreaming? But Alan quickly realised that there was no denying it – it was exactly who he thought it was. The two of them locked eyes, and with a knowing, cheeky smile, the man on the stairs nodded at Alan and walked off. The man's name was John Constantine. He is tall and likes to wear trench coats and a red tie. Oh, and he doesn't exist.

John Constantine is a comic book character created by Alan and some colleagues. Yet somehow he was there, in the sandwich shop. Alan was gobsmacked. How had John come to life?

Now, if we look at this logically, the character didn't come to life. It must have been a case of mistaken identity. But this is where the story gets weird. Alan wasn't the only person to see John Constantine. In fact, over the next few years, many of Alan's fellow comic book writers would report seeing him too. There was Peter Milligan, who said he bumped into Constantine at a party. Unlike Alan, he actually ran after him and attempted to talk to him, but unfortunately Constantine somehow disappeared before Milligan managed to catch up to him. Then there was Brian Azzarello, who suddenly saw Constantine at a bar in Chicago; he didn't approach him, though, as he was too nervous to say hi. And finally, Jamie Delano saw the comic book character strolling by the British Museum. They all believe they saw Constantine in real life – that he had jumped off the page. So what on earth is going on?

THE MYSTERIOUS CASE OF ARNOLD BOTTOMLEY

Fictional people coming to life has also been something of a problem for me recently. A while ago, an imaginary friend called Arnold Bottomley started appearing in my house. He first came into my life a few years ago when I was making up a bedtime story with my sons. In the story, a group of Earthlings were locked in a prison by an evil space villain. They were supposed to be saved by an intergalactic superhero, but when the tower door finally opened, instead there was some random guy who said, **'HELLO, I'M ARNOLD BOTTOMLEY.'**

We quickly kicked him out of the story, but every night he kept coming back, jumping into the story where he didn't belong. Always ruining the tale at a really exciting and important bit. 'Get out of here, Arnold Bottomley!' we would scream at him.

At first, I was very excited when Arnold Bottomley arrived in our lives. I never had an imaginary friend growing up. Which was horrible because my best friend did – he had a talking pig called Pogo. We all loved Pogo. He would come to dinner with us, watch movies in the cinema with us and join us on sleepovers. I couldn't see him, but that didn't matter. He was real to my friend. Quite a few of my friends had imaginary pals. I felt left out. So, in order not to look like a weirdo, I made one up. That's right, I made up an imaginary friend. I gave him a name – Charlie. I drew pictures of him, and I created a back story for him. But the truth is, no matter how hard I tried, I couldn't get him to become a real imaginary friend. And it ended up being really hard work to convince my actual friends that he was a *real* imaginary friend. I kept getting details about him wrong and eventually my friends got suspicious and accused me of lying: 'You don't have an imaginary friend! You're just making one up.'

'I do. Look, there he is,' I said, pointing to the empty space of air next to me. But I could tell my friends didn't believe me. 'Yeah, well, your imaginary friend isn't real either!' I yelled back accusingly.

'GAH' yelled my friend, facing an empty space next to him. 'Cover your ears, Pogo. Don't listen to him.'

I knew at that moment that I would never have a childhood imaginary friend. Which is why it is so odd that, many years later, I find myself not only with my own adult imaginary friend, but one that I share with my sons. We can all see him. We can almost smell him, and I do genuinely think that if I really, really tried, I could think Arnold Bottomley into existence. But that is surely impossible, isn't it?

CAN AUTHORS BRING CHARACTERS INTO LIFE FOR REAL?

If Arnold Bottomley seems real to me, imagine how real characters like Harry Potter or the Gruffalo must seem to their creators. Enid Blyton, who wrote *The Famous Five* and *The Magic Faraway Tree*, said she could hear her characters talking in her head as she was writing them. And she's not the only one. A study that surveyed 181 authors found that 114 of them heard their characters speaking, and not only that, but they were making their own decisions about what they were doing in the story.

I asked Robin Stevens, author of the *Murder Most Unladylike* series, if she experienced this too. 'Oh yes, absolutely! I can hear them talk, for sure. I might start them off by saying something, but then it's like I'm watching a movie in my head with them responding to each other. I can also watch them move around a room and feel the emotions they're feeling during the scene.'

Robin has never met her characters, but she can't shake the feeling that they are alive somewhere. 'I can't genuinely believe they're not real,' she said. 'It's mind-blowing to me that I couldn't go meet them. I feel like they're living in another country, maybe? But we're friends, and we chat all the time.'

Another author, Bec Hill, who wrote *Horror Heights: The Slime,* created a character that was a big, loveable, gooey green monster called Big Yikes. Big Yikes started as kind and cute, but as it grew bigger, it became more sinister, and Bec ended up having terrible nightmares in which Big Yikes was coming for her!

Some authors even had imaginary friends who would help them to write their books, like crime writer Agatha Christie. She had imaginary friends from a young age and she always spoke to them, even when she was over seventy years old. They kept her company, helped encourage her when she needed help and told her she could finish the books she was writing.

THE BUMPER LIST OF IMPOSSIBLE PEOPLE

Imaginary friends aren't the only impossible people who are reported to be walking among us. All over the world, people are constantly reporting strange encounters.
I've been keeping a running list of who to look for in my **YOGIBOGEYBOOK**, and you should too. So far the list goes:

1. IMMORTALS — people who live forever

2. FICTIONAL PEOPLE WHO HAVE COME TO LIFE

3. VAMPIRES

4. SUPERHUMAN MUMS

5. POTATOES ON THE RUN

(OK, I admit that number 5 is a bit of a weird one, but this made it on to the list after a friend of mine told me that his two best buddies swear on their lives that one night, while they were driving in the countryside, a potato with legs ran across the road in front of them.)

My dream is to spot one of these impossible people, and whenever I'm sitting in a restaurant or a café, or on a train or bus, and I have time to spare that I don't want to spend just staring at the back of people's heads trying to make them turn around, I always like to take out my **YOGIBOGEYBOOK** and flip to this list.

ARE THERE IMMORTALS?

Over the centuries, many people have spent their lives obsessing over the idea of immortality. They've often thought they can do this by discovering an 'elixir of life', which is effectively some item or potion that will make them live forever. The first emperor of China believed he had found the elixir of life, but unfortunately he was wrong. It turned out to be mercury, which is a very poisonous substance, and ironically, it reportedly killed him.

One person who is said to have achieved it is a man whose name you may be familiar with from the first *Harry Potter* book, and that is Nicolas Flamel. Flamel was actually a real person, not a made-up character for the book. He was a French scribe who was born in 1330 and has become a legendary figure thanks to the rumour that he had created something called the philosopher's stone, which would grant anyone who had it everlasting life. The official account of Flamel's life says that he died in 1418, but then 200 years later a book appeared that claimed to be written by a Nicolas Flamel himself, in which he wrote about the discovery of the stone. Scholars all generally agree that this must be a hoax. However, the legend has stuck, and it is said that Nicolas Flamel walks the Earth to this day!

DO VAMPIRES WALK AMONG US?

Nobody knows for sure if vampires exist, but according to a survey, if they do, the number one place in America for them to live is New York City. The survey, which took in data from 500 cities in America, found that because of the number of blood banks (vampires love blood), basement apartments (vampires hate the sun) and lack of garlic festivals (apparently that is a thing), vampires would love New York. And not only that, the city seems to be very accepting of vampires; it even has vampire-friendly clubs, and a lot of casket makers.

I've never personally seen a vampire. But perhaps the greatest account of someone having to deal with one belongs to one of the world's founding fathers of alien hunting: Frank Drake.

I mentioned Drake earlier in chapter 3. Remember him? He was the founder of SETI (the Search for Extra-Terrestrial Intelligence) and an important figure in the hunt for life in the universe. He was responsible for setting up multiple radio telescopes, which were pointed to the stars in the hope of one day receiving a message from aliens.

According to Drake, his job of being an alien hunter was once interrupted, because he had to become a vampire hunter for a few days instead.

One day, while he was scanning the skies for alien signals, one of the security team working at the satellite dish reported that he had seen a man with a black cloak skulking around. He looked like a vampire! *But vampires don't exist,* thought Drake, and he ignored the problem. Then, a few days later, a cow was found dead in a local farm, and a lot of its blood was missing, as if the blood had been drunk by something (or someone). Once word got out about this, many of Drake's staff started to freak out, and more and more vampire sightings were reported. Drake, despite not believing in vampires, had no choice but to do something about it. He researched how to rid an area of vampires, even calling up a vampire-bat expert for advice. The advice he received was simple: get everyone to eat lots of garlic. That usually deters vampires in the books. So Drake arranged for all meals served from the observatory kitchen to include garlic. It worked! No more vampires were seen in the area. And Frank Drake returned to the less weird task of hunting aliens again.

SUPERHUMAN MUMS

The last major category on the list in my **YOGIBOGEYBOOK** is probably the most achievable. Superhuman mums!

Is there such a thing as a superhuman? In my years of looking I have read about many examples, but none of the stories appear to be verified.

If there are superhumans out there, then they sure seem to have a knack for only using their superhuman powers whenever there is no one around to see it.

I feel sorry for superhumans who only manage to achieve incredible things when no one is looking. They have to go around for the rest of their lives promising that something happened but with no proof. It's like what Dr Irving Finkel once told me: 'Science needs something to happen every time for it to be accepted as fact. But what if it only happens once?' This exact problem is something that was once experienced by a super-mum.

Many years ago, a mother walked out of her house in search of her wandering child and was immediately faced with her worst nightmare. Her baby had somehow crawled towards the road and become trapped under the back of a parked car. Rather than scream and panic, she went into hero mode and, summoning all her strength (or possibly superpowers), she picked the back of the car up, allowing the baby to crawl free. Amazing! Think about any adult you know – do you think they could lift a car? I tried it today, and I can report that it was impossible. There's no way anyone I know could lift a car. So who was this super-mum? Sadly, she has become a sort of urban legend, and no one seems to know her name. And what's worse, she must have spent the rest of her life telling everyone that she had lifted a car, only to have no one believe her. It is often the curse of doing something impossible. No one believes you!

NOTE TO SELF: Make sure to ask the car's owner next time. That guy was NOT happy with me!

Except . . . we do believe her. You see, sometimes, someone else is there to see the impossible happen. And this was one of those times. Just a little down the road from the trapped baby was a man called Jack. He watched as the mother lifted up the car and rescued her baby. And then he had an idea. 'This woman proved to me that an ordinary person in desperate circumstances can . . . do things that they wouldn't ordinarily do.' Inspired by what he witnessed, Jack made it into art and transformed the super-mum into a character who would become known by children across the world as part of the biggest movie franchise of all time. The man on the road that day was called Jack Kirby, the illustrator for Marvel Comics, and he would turn this superhero mother into his next character. First he made her green, and then he gave this green monster a name: the Incredible Hulk!

HOW TO SOLVE A PROBLEM LIKE ARNOLD BOTTOMLEY

So far I have still not managed to meet any of the impossible people on my **YOGIBOGEYBOOK** list. Well, except for one. Because I swear I can almost properly see Arnold Bottomley. So much so that it's beginning to be a problem. Recently, my son Wilf asked me at breakfast, 'Dad, how do we get rid of Arnold Bottomley?' I looked up from my bowl of cereal and saw Wilf's worried face. Most kids would love for their imaginary friends to suddenly become real. Imagine that, a best friend who could travel with you everywhere, play with you all day long. But Wilf doesn't want that, and I know exactly why –

it's because his imaginary friend is really, *really* annoying. I mean a total butt nugget. As I said earlier, the guy will not stop ruining the endings of our stories! Just when you think something amazing is going to happen, in he pops. 'Who are you?' we yell at the stranger in our story.

'I'm Arnold Bottomley!' Gosh, it's annoying.

'So, how do we get rid of Arnold?' asked Wilf.

'Hmm . . . How do you get rid of an imaginary friend? I guess we could sell him on eBay,' I replied. I had read about someone selling an imaginary friend called Jon Malipieman for thousands of pounds on eBay. The listing read:

> **My imaginary friend Jon Malipieman is getting too old for me now . . . and I feel I am growing out of him. He is very friendly. Along with him, I will send you what he likes and dislikes along with his favourite things to do and his personal self-portrait.**

31 people bid for him!

'But are you sure you want to get rid of him?' I asked Wilf. As much as I found Arnold Bottomley a nuisance too, I had read about the benefits of having an imaginary friend. 'What if HE ends up protecting us? It might be good to have an invisible friend around.'

You see, kids aren't the only people who have invisible friends. Often, many of the most brave and adventurous explorers on Earth have found themselves at their worst moments being visited by an imaginary friend. These visitors are known as the 'Third Man'.

The first report of a Third Man comes from one of the great British Antarctic explorers, Ernest Shackleton. The story goes that Shackleton and two other explorers were out on an expedition in the Antarctic tundra when they found themselves exhausted, hungry and nearing death. It was then that Shackleton noticed something: 'It seemed to me often that we were four, not three.' Shackleton noticed one extra person in their party. An imaginary fourth person who had appeared out of nowhere.

And he wasn't the only one. Many people have looked into this phenomenon, and there is no shortage of explorers willing to admit that they have been visited in moments of desperation by someone who shouldn't have been there.

IMAGINARY FRIENDS ARE REALLY ANNOYING

In 1933, the mountain climber Frank Smythe was so convinced he had been joined on Mount Everest by an invisible friend that when he pulled out some Kendal Mint Cake from his pocket for a quick bite to eat, he snapped it in half to offer a piece to this other person!

The first woman to ski across the Antarctic, explorer Ann Bancroft, has experienced it too, when she was exhausted on an expedition. Someone, who wasn't supposed to be there, had appeared to keep her company in this darkest of moments.

And it's not just explorers who have reported it. During his record-breaking 33-hour solo flight over the Atlantic from New York to Paris in 1927, Charles Lindbergh reported that he had multiple imaginary friends in the plane beside him. They kept him company, and some even gave him directions.

Are our imaginary friends becoming real people in our greatest times of need? Scientists believe our brains are creating these people who aren't supposed to be there as a way of helping us cope with the bad situation we find ourselves in.

The thing is, once these explorers were out of danger, their imaginary friends went away, and once kids grow up, their imaginary friends disappear too. Which is why

I made a trip to New York, to stand outside number 12 Gay Street. It was to marvel at the one place I know of that an imaginary friend is said to have remained ...

THE GHOST OF THE SHADOW

Ever since the 1920s, residents at 12 Gay Street have reported experiencing bizarre and unexplainable things. Footsteps were heard on the staircase when there was no one there, objects moved on their own in neighbouring rooms, the dog would bark at invisible things in the corner of the room, and several people claimed to have seen a figure walking the corridors dressed in a top hat and black clothes.

Eventually, the house gained such a reputation for its mysterious goings on that the celebrated ghost hunter Hans Holzer decided to pay it a visit. He wrote about it in a book called *Yankee Ghosts*.

Holzer's book eventually found its way into the hands of an author called Walter B. Gibson, who was stunned when he read the tale. 'That's not a ghost!' he immediately realised. 'That's my imaginary creation.'

Walter was an insatiable author. He was always writing, and he used to type so fast and for so long that his fingers would swell up into giant sausage-looking things. But even then, he kept typing.

The most popular thing Gibson ever wrote concerned a character he created called the Shadow, a vigilante alter ego of the main character, Lamont Cranston. Gibson became so obsessed with this character that as he wrote more and more about him, he started to feel he had come alive. Gibson started to visualise his character walking through the halls of his house. He could see him as he wrote, dressed in a black suit and top hat. Oh, and the address that Gibson wrote a lot of these books in was 12 Gay Street.

Is it possible that Gibson's imaginary friend became so real to him that he somehow burst into real life? And that when Gibson left the house, the shadow of the character remained, continuing to walk the halls forever more? Is he still there today?

It's an odd and exciting thought. Are there houses around the world where you'll find Harry Potter, Mary Poppins and Oliver Twist walking up and down the staircases and making objects move? I'd quite like to meet some of those characters, if so.

CHAPTER 8
IS IT RUDE TO GIFT SOMEONE A CURSED ITEM?

A few years ago, I was making my way home on the train when a sudden, terrifying thought hit me. I started to sweat profusely. I had made a **HUGE** mistake. In my bag I had something that I had forgotten had been banned from ever entering my house. What was I thinking? The banned item was a book, but this was not any normal book. It was a book that was rumoured to be **CURSED** and would bring bad luck to anyone who possessed a copy of it. And it was written by someone who many believed to be a real-life evil British wizard – like He Who Shall Not Be Named in the *Harry Potter* books. And just like those books, I'm afraid I cannot reveal his name either. So, let's call him He Who Shall Also Not Be Named instead.

Now, as an Impossible Investigator, I am fascinated by things that are thought to bring people bad luck, because surely bad luck doesn't exist? However, there is no denying the incalculable influence it has had on the people of our world. And it can manifest in many different ways. Sometimes it can be a number (like the number 13), sometimes it can be an action (like breaking a mirror, or stepping under a ladder, or opening an umbrella while indoors) and sometimes it can be an object (like, say, a cursed book written by an evil wizard).

Perhaps the weirdest of all is that sometimes it can be a person.

CAN PEOPLE BE CURSED?

For some years now I have been putting together an **IMPOSSIBLE DICTIONARY**, where, instead of providing a written definition of the words, each entry shows a picture of something that best defines it. (I had this idea after my school friend Zamir once told me that if I looked up the word STUPID in the dictionary, I would see a picture of me! He was wrong, though; I wasn't there when I looked.)

If you were to look up the term 'bad luck' in the **IMPOSSIBLE DICTIONARY**, you would see a picture of American park ranger Roy Sullivan, AKA the Spark Ranger.

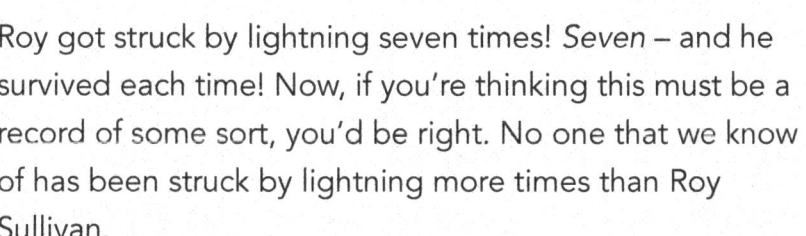

Roy Sullivan used to catch fire so often that he had to carry a can of water wherever he went so that he could put himself out. The reason Roy kept catching fire is because the guy couldn't stop getting struck by lightning.

Roy got struck by lightning seven times! *Seven* – and he survived each time! Now, if you're thinking this must be a record of some sort, you'd be right. No one that we know of has been struck by lightning more times than Roy Sullivan.

The first time he was hit, he was fleeing from a burning watchtower that had already been struck by lightning. He shouldn't have survived that, and he vowed never to be out in open land again during a storm. Instead, he'd take shelter somewhere that lightning can't hit. Like inside a truck.

The second time he was hit by lightning he was inside a truck. This should be impossible; the truck acts as a giant metal shell to protect those inside it. Unfortunately, Roy had left a window open, and the lightning came through the crack, singeing his eyebrows off and setting his hair on fire.

After the third and fourth time, Roy came to believe he was cursed, and that some bigger force was out to get him. And his friends agreed with him. Anytime they were with him and a storm started brewing in the distance, they would quickly make their excuses and skedaddle out of there as fast as possible.

By the fifth time, Roy had become so convinced the clouds were now actively following him that he started trying to outrun them when he saw them in the distance. But they kept following him. Fortunately, he made it to his vehicle and after making sure the windows were all shut, he prepared to wait out the storm. Once he was sure the storm had passed, he got out of the truck and was immediately hit by a bolt of lightning so strong it blew his shoe off his foot.

The sixth time it was the same. Roy spotted a cloud and, according to him, it spotted him back. It then effectively chased him as he ran off before finally shooting lightning at him and setting his head on fire again.

The seventh and final time Roy was hit by lightning coincided with another ridiculous milestone for the cursed Spark Ranger: it happened moments before he found himself having to fight a bear for the twenty-second time. Roy had just been struck by lightning when suddenly the bear appeared, and Roy had to beat him away with a stick, all while his hair was aflame.

Has anyone suffered more consistent bad luck than Roy Sullivan?

Frane Selak would probably come a close second, to be fair. Selak was cursed with bad luck too. He couldn't stop getting into accidents. It all started with a train crash, which he somehow survived but which scared him enough to avoid trains for a while. The next year, Selak took his first ever plane ride; unfortunately the plane's door ripped open mid-flight and Selak was sucked out of the door and plunged miles to the ground. He somehow survived by managing to land on a haystack. Deciding never to fly again, he got on a bus, which immediately shot off a bridge into a river. Finally, he decided that cars would be safest, and what do you think happened? Yep, the car caught fire, burning all the hair off his head! At this point, he decided that transport was far too dangerous for him and decided to just walk . . . but was then hit by a bus.

After all this bad luck, Selak thought he might as well go back to cars. But that didn't work out too well when his car flew off the side of a mountain after he collided with another vehicle. Fortunately, he was able to leap from the car in time and hang on to a tree on the side of the cliff.

That is one unlucky guy. But the only reason he doesn't beat Roy Sullivan in becoming the face of 'bad luck' in the **IMPOSSIBLE DICTIONARY** is that (A) none of his stories were ever independently verified and (B) Selak's luck finally changed. After all these accidents he went on to **WIN THE LOTTERY!**

IS THIRTEEN AN UNLUCKY NUMBER?

When I arrived home with the cursed book in my bag, I set about making a plan. We had a garden out the back. *That's not in the house*, I thought. All I needed to do was walk down the side alley of my house, and as long as my wife, Fenella, didn't catch me, I could leave the book at the back of the garden in a plastic bag, and then occasionally sneak out to read it. Unfortunately, as I passed the kitchen window that looks out into the alley, Fenella caught me.

'What are you doing?' she asked through the windowpane. I didn't want to lie, so I explained that technically this wasn't the house. 'Are you nuts?' she said. 'In what universe is the garden not part of our house? You actually think I'm going to let you keep a book by He Who Shall Also Not Be Named in our garden?'

Fenella told me to go out the front and throw it in the bin. But I didn't want to throw it away, and instead I knocked on my neighbour's door.

'Hi, Dan,' said my neighbour JP. 'How can I help?'

'Is it OK if I keep this book in your house? Fenella doesn't want it in our house because she says it's cursed.'

'Sure thing,' said JP.

JP's house was number 12, and ours was number 14. We both lucked out, because if it was number 13 our houses might be worth less. And that's because many people believe the number 13 to be cursed. Real estate agents have reported that houses at number 13 are historically listed lower thanks to this superstition. Which is so bizarre. Thirteen is a completely normal, completely harmless number. Or is it? People are so afraid of it that often buildings won't include a thirteenth floor. And many aeroplanes don't have a row 13, either. There are even accounts of how in restaurants in France, if exactly 13 guests are to be seated at a table, someone known as the *quatorze* is brought in to make the number of diners up to 14. There are numerous stories of the curse of number 13, but perhaps none greater than the third mission to the Moon.

On 11 April 1970, Apollo 13 launched into space. Many commented on the unlucky number in their mission, but NASA were not bothered. In fact, they sort of teased those people who did believe it was unlucky by launching the spaceship at 13.13. Two days later, the curse of 13 appeared to strike. On 13 April there was a critical explosion in the spaceship, after one of the three crew, Jack Swigert, flipped a switch as part of a routine task. Swigert was the thirteenth astronaut to go to the Moon with the Apollo space program. Fortunately, through incredibly quick thinking and ingenuity, Apollo 13 made it safely home, but many believed that none of the problems would have happened if they had just skipped 13 and launched Apollo 14 instead.

Not everyone fears the number 13, though. Like the members of the Thirteen Club in America, founded in 1882. The club, which was made up of 13 men, would always meet on Friday the thirteenth at 7.13 p.m. To make things as unlucky as possible for each guest, they had to get to the dinner table by walking under a ladder. They then sat around a big table chatting, eating and breaking dozens of small mirrors, while surrounded by open umbrellas. The club eventually grew to over 500 members, but they were always seated in groups of 13.

Another number people get terrified of is 666. This is the number associated with the Devil and is thought to be evil. As a result, Tuesday 6 June 2006 (06/06/06) became one of the more feared days in modern history, particularly to people who were on the brink of giving birth. Hundreds of expectant mothers desperately tried not to give birth on the 'day of the devil'. One person who didn't care, though, was Suzanne Cooper of Bristol. She was not only happy to deliver her baby that day, but was also totally unfazed when she delivered a baby boy weighing 6lb 6oz during the hour of 6 a.m. They named the boy Damien, which was the name of the devil's son in a popular 1970s movie.

CAN OBJECTS BE CURSED?

The morning after dropping my cursed book at my neighbour JP's house, I bumped into him in the street. 'How's it going?' I asked.

'Terrible,' he replied.

Apparently, after I dropped off the book, JP had to go out for the night, leaving the book in the house with his wife, Kate. Kate then decided to look up who He Who Shall Also Not Be Named was. When JP returned hours later, he found Kate shaking in fear under the blankets in their bed. **'GET THAT BOOK OUT OF OUR HOUSE!'** she yelled.

'So where is it?' I asked JP.

'I immediately took it out to the garden shed,' he replied. And that, my Impossible Investigators, is where it remained.

I was utterly fascinated by how strongly everyone was buying into this supposed curse. It was just a normal book! There were tens of thousands of copies of it all over the world. But when we collectively believe something is bad luck, then it gets taken very seriously. Cursed items are dotted all over the planet, and I always make sure to write down exactly where they are in my **YOGIBOGEYBOOK** so I can visit them one day. (Fenella likes this list too, as it shows her exactly where to stay away from.)

EXTRACT FROM THE YOGIBOGEYBOOK #5

LIST OF CURSED ITEMS TO VISIT

1. THE CURSED JEWEL – Where: Natural History Museum, London

Sitting behind a glass cabinet in the mineralogy department of London's Natural History Museum is a cursed jewel. Known as the Cursed Amethyst, it was acquired by the museum from an owner who was so fearful of it, he had it locked away in a bank, leaving instructions for it not to be removed until 3 years after his death.

The stone, which was originally housed in the Temple of Indra, in Kanpur, India, was stolen by a soldier named Colonel Ferris, who brought it back to England. Soon after his return to Britain, he got ill and died. The stone was then passed on to his son, who suffered the same fate, and so it was passed on to his friend, who died too.

The stone then found its way to a writer called Edward Heron-Allen, who suffered such bad luck after acquiring it that he decided to get rid of it once and for all by throwing it into a canal. Three months later, the jewel found its way back to his door after being found by someone dredging the canal who knew it belonged to Heron-Allen. Realising he couldn't get rid of this thing, he finally put it in a box, locked it, put it in another box, and then another, like a giant wooden pass the parcel. The stone was then locked in a bank's safe. Three years after his death, Heron-Allen's box was removed by his daughter with the instructions that it should be donated to the Natural History Museum, along with a letter that read: 'Whoever shall then open it, shall first read out this warning, and then do as he pleases with the jewel. My advice to him or her is to cast it into the sea.'

The staff accepted the donation, and it is now displayed to the public (though do double check that before visiting, as the museum often changes its exhibits!). No one has since reported any weird curses from it, and in fact the stone has become something of a famous item among curators of the museum, who believe that the story was just made up by Heron-Allen and that no curse ever existed. Rumour has it that it is often taken out of its case for the museum staff's annual Halloween party.

THE CURSE THAT KEEPS COMING BACK

2. THE CURSED AEROPLANE – Where: National Museum of the United States Air Force

In 1943, an American military plane called the *Lady Be Good* went missing while on a combat mission during the Second World War. It was thought to have crashed into the ocean, but 15 years later was found in the Libyan Desert by a team of geologists. The plane was empty and still in good shape considering its years in the desert, but with no crew to be found. Because it was in such good condition, the plane was brought back to a base and taken apart, and then many of the parts were used on other aircraft. All sounds normal and fine, right? This is when things started to go weird.

The first plane to experience problems had been fitted with the *Lady Be Good*'s transmitter. As it was making its way to land, it mysteriously suffered some propeller difficulties and only just made it down safely after various items from inside were lobbed out to help with the weight of the plane. Next, there was a plane that had been refitted with the radio receiver: this plane wasn't so lucky, and sadly crashed into the Mediterranean. And finally, there was the plane that had been fitted with one of the armrests from the *Lady Be Good*, which went down in the Gulf of Sidra. The plane was never fully recovered, though much later, when some items from it washed up on the shore. There wasn't much, but one thing they did find . . . was the armrest from the *Lady Be Good*.

3. THE CURSED TREE – Where: Alton, England

Usually when a branch falls from a tree, no one notices. It never makes the press, and it almost certainly doesn't require the Earl of Shrewsbury to confirm that no members of his family had died. However, for 200 years now, there is one tree that has always got media attention. This is the tale of the Chained Oak.

The story goes that one night, sometime in the 1800s, the Earl of Shrewsbury was on his way home in his carriage when an old woman jumped in front of his path, causing the horses to grind to an immediate halt. The old woman asked the Earl for a coin, but the Earl refused, demanding she go away. This angered the woman, and so she told the Earl she would place a curse on him and his family.

Pointing to the tall oak tree that stood next to him, she announced that every time a branch from that tree fell, a member of his family would die. Later that night, Alton was hit by a storm. It caused a branch to fall from the tree, and a member of the Earl's family suddenly died.

This terrified the Earl. To prevent a branch from ever falling again, he had the tree chained up. There are still chains on the tree to this day. No one can be sure if the story is true, but neither does anyone have a good explanation for how the chains got there.

Next time you visit Alton Towers and go on a ride they call Hex, just know that it is based on the story of the Chained Oak.

4. THE CURSED INSTRUMENT – Where: The Franklin Institute in Philadelphia

Benjamin Franklin was a remarkable person. A founding father of America, he was also responsible for many inventions – including the lightning rod (something Roy Sullivan could have done with), bifocals (which allow people who need help seeing far away and up close to use just one pair of glasses) and he was almost the inventor of a perfume for your bottom – so that all our farts could smell better. But I think he ran out of time on that one. Strangest of all, though, was the fact that he was accused of having invented something impossible: an instrument that could kill you when you listened to it!

Franklin invented the glass armonica, which is basically an organ that is played using water and glass. You know that trick some people do where they run their fingers around the top of a glass and it produces a musical note? Well, it's sort of like that, but on a much bigger scale. To begin with the instrument proved popular with composers like Beethoven and Mozart, who both wrote music using them. But then rumours started going around that this instrument wasn't all that it seemed. Stories of people going mad when listening to the songs it played started circulating. Women were fainting, dogs were going wild, young girls were reportedly screaming in their sleep after hearing it, and some people were even reported to have died. The worries about this cursed instrument became so great that places started banning it. With such bad press, the instrument quickly went out of fashion and was rarely seen again.

SO, WHATEVER HAPPENED TO THE CURSED BOOK?

A year had passed since I committed the huge *faux pas* of putting a cursed book into the hands of my neighbour, when we got the sad news that JP and his family were moving out. I don't think it was because of the book, though we did all come to suspect that the garden was haunted (but that's another very long story I won't go into!) As the leaving day neared, I visited JP to relieve his shed of the cursed book. However, when he went to get it, he discovered

that it wasn't where he left it. He searched and searched, but it wasn't to be found. 'No one goes into that shed but me,' he said. 'It can't have moved!'

And to this day it remains a mystery. We have no idea what happened to the book by He Who Shall Also Not Be Named.

As for me, I had learned my lesson in toying with cursed items around those who believe they might have power. And to make sure of never doing something like this again, I set about giving myself a reminder. Until further notice, if you flip open my **IMPOSSIBLE DICTIONARY** and look up the definition of **'STUPID'**, what you'll find is a picture of me.

CHAPTER 9
DID DINOSAURS BEAT US TO THE MOON?

It was 11 p.m. – waaaaay past bedtime – and I was on New King Street in Bath, leaning against a house and looking up at the sky. It's such a normal-looking street. But it was right there on that spot, in the very house I was leaning against, that on 13 March 1781 a scientist called William Herschel became the first person to spot Uranus! (Stop sniggering.) No one had seen Uranus before. Imagine that, being the first person to see one of the eight planets in our solar system.

(We used to have nine planets in the Solar System when I was a kid, but the ninth one, Pluto, got downgraded after the tireless work of a scientist who online goes by the name PLUTOKILLER.)

Now, I think we can all agree that Uranus is an incredibly silly name for a planet. But it's not Herschel's fault. He originally wanted to call it George. So we might have had Earth, Mercury, Mars, Jupiter, Venus, Saturn, Neptune and George! George's Star, to give it its full proposed name, would have been in tribute to King George III. However, other astronomers rejected the suggestion: 'GEORGE? You want to call it GEORGE?! No, no. It needs a respectable name, something that no one would ever find funny or snigger at in the playground. We shall call it URANUS.' And no one has ever made fun of it since . . .

Back then, Uranus was nothing more than a dot in the sky to Herschel. These days, however, we know so much more about it. For example, when it rains on the planet, it rains diamonds! Oh, and its atmosphere consists of a lot of hydrogen sulphide (and stinks like rotten eggs) which means the clouds of Uranus smell like farts.

It's now over 200 years since Herschel died in 1822. He lived to be eighty-three, and died just 3 months before his eighty-forth birthday. Coincidentally, it takes Uranus 83.75 years to orbit the Sun – and, as I stand on the street where Uranus was discovered, I can't help but think about all the things we have achieved in the last two centuries that Herschel would have thought impossible. Like aeroplanes! Which were first made a reality by the Wright brothers in 1903.

For thousands of years flying vehicles were dreamed about, but everyone thought they were impossible. In fact, just 9 weeks before the Wright brothers flew a plane for the first time ever in 1903, the New York Times newspaper published their prediction of when a flying machine would finally be invented. They estimated it to be some time in the next 1 to 10 million years.

Now, they're everywhere. In fact, at any given time there are roughly 10,000 planes flying somewhere in the sky. This means that on average, right now, there are almost ten times as many people flying in the sky as there are living in the city of Bath.

BATH POPULATION: 110,000

SKY POPULATION: Over 1,000,000

If you were able to tell your great-great-great grandparent this, they would think you were going loopy.

While I think about it, I want to quickly acknowledge a problem with being an Impossible Investigator – that it involves a lot of travel. It's all very well, I can hear you say, telling us we should go and live with time travellers in Italy or go Yeti hunting in Bhutan, but the truth is that getting to somewhere like Peru when you live in, say, Dorking is not very likely. The good news is that there is a place available to you, far bigger than the Earth, with plenty more **IMPOSSIBLE THINGS** to investigate, and all you need to do is look up. Well, leave the house first, unless you have an incredibly interesting bedroom ceiling, of course. Space is infinitely large, and there is never a dull night.

I love staring at the sky at night. At home I have a special space chair (it's just a normal chair, but it definitely sounds cooler when you say space chair), which I keep by a window so I can look out every night. As a kid I used to see if I could spot a UFO, or a shooting star, or a supernova (a very rare event where a star explodes!). It's so bizarre to think that most of the stars in the sky that we are looking at are probably not there any more and died long ago, but we can still see them because the light they emit has taken millions of years to reach us. I often like to look for the Mizar and Alcor stars. These two stars were very important in ancient Greece, as they were used by army generals to test the eyesight of potential soldiers and determine what job was best for them. The two stars are very close to each other in the night sky, and supposedly if you could see Alcor separate from Mizar, it meant you had good eyesight and you could become an archer in the army. But if you couldn't, you'd have to find another job, like, I dunno, cheese fortune teller (which used to be a job back then: you would sit in the streets predicting people's futures by studying a lump of cheese. Actually that sounds great).

From our earthly vantage point, it's an exciting time to be alive – we are currently living in the Stelliferous Era of the universe, which basically means when you look up at the night sky, there are stars shining for us to see. Right now, the lights are still on for us in the universe. But one day, as the universe continues to expand, the stars will die, and we will no longer see their light.

NOTE TO SELF: Consult the cheddar in the fridge when I'm home tonight.

I keep a big list of the **IMPOSSIBLE THINGS TO LOOK FOR IN SPACE** in my **YOGIBOGEYBOOK**. And while I was standing there trying to spot Uranus (seriously, stop sniggering), I thought about some of the other things you should be on the lookout for too.

IMPOSSIBLE THINGS TO LOOK FOR IN SPACE

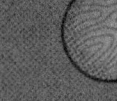

Firstly, there are the **THINGS THAT ARE FALLING TO EARTH.**

Have you ever seen a shooting star? When a shooting star makes its way to the ground, it is called a meteorite. Meteorites fall to Earth all the time. One estimate has it that about 17,000 meteorites hit us every year. And they can be very valuable, so there are plenty of meteorite hunters out there who keep their eyes trained to the sky, ready to get in their car, or even on a plane, as soon as one crashes to Earth. One meteorite hunter I spoke to keeps a suitcase packed at all times so that he can make a quick escape should the need arise. He'll be out at dinner, see a meteorite streak through the air and quickly dash out of there like he's Batman. (Meteorites can be hard to identify, and often are confused with normal Earth rocks. When a meteorite is mistaken to be a rock from space, but later found out to be just a normal rock from Earth, geologists call it a meteorwrong.)

It used to be different; we used to be scared of things falling from space. In fact, just over a hundred years ago, many thought that a rock from space was going to end the world.

HALLEY'S COMET PILLS

On 19 May 1910, tens of thousands of people around the world prepared themselves for an apocalypse. This happened after some newspapers published a story claiming that a scientist called Camille Flammarion had said the Earth was going to be passing through the tail of Halley's comet, and that this was very bad news! Apparently the millions-of-miles-long comet tail had been analysed, and it was discovered that it contained cyanide, a deadly poison. This meant that as Earth passed through it, it would poison us all.

Now, the strange thing is, this isn't true. In fact, Camille Flammarion never said this. In an interview he gave about the comet he said it would not hurt us. However, he did mention what would happen if it did have the ability to hurt us, and for some reason that's the only bit everyone remembers.

As a result, there was mass panic. People gathered in St Peter's Square in Vatican City to prepare for the end of the world. In Europe, churches left their doors open so congregations could gather to pray. Meanwhile, others thought they could stop the poison getting to them by sealing up their chimneys and any holes in their homes (like keyholes in the door) to stop it from coming through. Perhaps oddest of all, in London fake medicine merchants went around selling 'Halley's Comet Pills', which promised to protect you against the intergalactic poison. Needless to say, the panic was all for nothing. Humanity survived!

THE MYSTERIOUS STAR JELLY

There are many things thought to have been carried to Earth via meteorites. As we've seen in chapter 3, many people have speculated that life might have begun thanks to biological matter being carried from another world and crash landing on Earth. Others have suggested Venus flytraps are aliens: these odd-looking plants were thought to be from another planet, largely because it was noticed that they were only growing naturally in the marshes of North and South Carolina, a place thought to be a meteorite crash site. But scientists are adamant there is nothing alien about them. And it later turned out not to be a meteor crater either. However, there is one enduring mystery that hasn't been solved, and that is a curious substance known as star jelly.

There is a mysterious goo that keeps popping up in fields around the world that has been reported on for over 700 years now, and we still have no idea what it is. Those who have seen

it say that not long after spotting it, it would evaporate. It goes by many names: star slime, star slubber, star spurt, but is most commonly known as star jelly. What is it? Some say it comes from alien galaxies, while others say it could be frog eggs. Some people also think that the substance can be used to communicate with the dead. Or perhaps it is a mutant monster created by industrial factories? This last idea came about when, in 1950, some policemen in Philadelphia discovered a six-foot mound of star jelly in the streets. When they attempted to pick it up, it dissolved in front of their eyes. It was noted that this batch of jelly was found within half a mile of a gas factory. (This is possibly the most infamous batch of star-jelly, as it got turned into a famous horror movie called *The Blob*.)

What's mad is that we just don't know what it is. Star jelly first gained its reputation for coming from outer space following many reports that people had come across it following a meteor shower. Like in 1996, in Hobart, Tasmania, when a meteor was reported in the sky. The next day, star jelly was said to have been seen on the streets and gardens of the city.

Sounds impossible, right? Star jelly is definitely on my Christmas list next year. I'd also love to get my hands on a rock that landed in France just over a decade ago.

THE IMPOSSIBLE ROCK

In 2011, a 4.57-billion-year-old space rock crashed through the roof of a home in Paris. This is an extremely rare occurrence – scientists reckon that in the last 400 years, only 50 meteorites have actually crashed in France.

This is an impossible object I wish I could speak to – I want to tell it whose house it crashed into. And watch as it replies, 'Noooooo waaaaay.' Because out of a population of over 2 million people, the space rock happened to crash into the house of a family called . . . the Comettes!

Meteorites are incredibly valuable and can fetch huge sums of money, but the Comette family decided not to sell. No money could ever be as valuable as the moment the Comettes' son, Hugo, brought his own comet into school for show and tell.

IMPOSSIBLE THINGS ORBITING THE PLANET

Next to keep your eye out for are the **IMPOSSIBLE THINGS** orbiting our planet. For example, if you stare at the night sky long enough, you will see moving lights, travelling really fast. These aren't UFOs – they're satellites. The first satellite, Sputnik, was launched in 1957, and since then there have been thousands more. (Including two I read about as kid that were built to chase each other, monitoring the distance between them. These satellites were known as Tom and Jerry.) However, I like to look out for one that most people think doesn't exist, an impossible one – a 13,000-year-old satellite called the Black Knight.

THE BLACK KNIGHT

The Black Knight satellite has had people hunting for it for years without success. Some say it is an alien satellite spying on us, while others think it was launched by a long-lost ancient civilisation on Earth. No one quite knows where the stories of the Black Knight originate from, but many claim to have seen this lonely ancient vessel flying across the night sky.

In 1998 a photo of the Black Knight satellite was released. Had it finally been proven that there was an ancient technology orbiting our planet? No, say the experts. That photo is actually of an astronaut's blanket that accidentally flew into space during a spacewalk.

And so the hunt continues for the Black Knight.

I do love looking into the night sky and thinking of the Black Knight, though. What if there was a lost ancient civilisation on Earth who had the technology to send a satellite into space, but then, like the dinosaurs, they were wiped out, and over time all evidence of their existence slowly rotted away, and all that was left was a lone satellite? I wonder if this could happen to us. Will humans be around in millions of years' time? What might they look like? Will one of them be a direct descendent of yours? Will we have cracked immortality by then or will we be extinct like the dinosaurs?

THE FIRST MAN-MADE SATELLITE

Another impossible item that some people believe may be orbiting our planet is what might be the first satellite to be sent by us into space. No, not Sputnik, but a manhole cover.

Just a few months before Sputnik was launched into space, scientists were testing out a big bomb. To do this, they dug a 400 feet deep hole, placed the bomb at the bottom and then covered the hole with cement and a manhole cover. The explosion was much larger than anyone anticipated, and the force of the bomb was so strong that it shot the manhole cover into the air at a speed of 130,000 mph (the fastest man-made object on Earth ever!). It was going so fast that the scientist running the experiment jokingly said in passing that it could have shot into space. We have no proof of that; however, one thing we do know is that no one has ever found the manhole cover since. Could it be orbiting our planet?

One remarkable thing that is definitely orbiting us – currently travelling around our planet at 17,135 mph an hour in a non-stop loop – is a giant six-bedroomed space house!

THE INTERNATIONAL SPACE STATION

Fitted with two bathrooms, a kitchen and a gym, the International Space Station has housed over 250 flatmates in its time and has been constantly travelling through space with astronauts inside since the year 2000.

What an amazing fact! No other civilisation in the history of Earth has been able to say that they've had a sleepover in space, and it's all thanks to our space programs. Even more amazing is the fact that 1 November 2000 was the last time that all of humankind was living on Earth at the same time! Ever since then there have always been between one and thirteen Earthlings living in space.

Wait, here's an even better fact: in 1991 there were 5.3 billion people on Earth and 60,000 jellyfish in space! (**ACTUAL SPACE JELLY!** This was part of an experiment to see how jellyfish coped when they lived in space: 2,478 were flown into space, and by the time the experiment had finished the jellyfish families had grown to that massive number. Hmmm . . . new theory: is it possible they escaped the space station and are orbiting Earth now, occasionally falling back onto the planet?)

The International Space Station is a fascinating experiment. It does weird things to the people who live in it, like making them forget about gravity when they come back to Earth. If you're drinking from a bottle of water in space, you can just let go of it when you're done and it will float instead of crashing to the ground. Astronauts often forget that doesn't happen back on Earth, so always remember to use the cheap mugs if an astronaut ever pops over for tea. This must cause havoc in the town of Pontefract in the UK, where several astronauts are known to spend time.

Astronauts living in the International Space Station are constantly working on solving mysteries. Sometimes they are big, like 'can we survive in space for long periods of time?' or they can be small, like 'what did I do with my tomato?' This was a question that Frank Rubio asked himself when he lost a tomato in space. He returned to Earth before he could find it, and it wasn't until 8 months later that an astronaut up in the International Space Station discovered a floating shrivelled tomato. Mystery solved.

Perhaps the oddest and most seemingly **IMPOSSIBLE THING** to happen up there is the time an astronaut almost drowned in space!

CAN YOU DROWN IN SPACE?

In 2013, Italian astronaut Luca Parmitano, who was living in the International Space Station, was 1 hour and 32 minutes into a 6.5-hour spacewalk when disaster struck. He noticed that water was accumulating inside his helmet. At first NASA's ground staff on Earth were not worried. But Parmitano was – the water was slowly filling up his helmet like a fishbowl. Where it was leaking into the helmet from, NASA still today aren't 100% sure, but they think it was a faulty cooling system in the spacesuit. By the time that NASA realised the problem was serious and ordered Parmitano back to the station, the water had almost filled his helmet. To make matters worse, the space station had now travelled far enough around the Earth that the Sun had set (because the International Space Station takes 90 minutes to travel around the world, it means that astronauts experience sixteen sunrises and sunsets every single day), and Parmitano couldn't see a thing. Using his memory of the layout of the spacecraft, Parmitano managed to make it back to the entry hatch, where a fellow astronaut opened his helmet to allow all the water – around five cups' worth – to come gushing out. Parmitano survived, but so nearly became the first astronaut living in the International Space Station to die in space. And what a weird cause of death it would have been: drowning.

IMPOSSIBLE THINGS BEYOND THE EARTH

Heading past the Earth's orbit now, and over to the Moon. Plenty of **IMPOSSIBLE THINGS** wait for us there.

History books will teach you that on 21 July 1969, American astronauts Neil Armstrong and Buzz Aldrin became the first Earthlings to stand on the Moon. But there is a theory that says this might not be true. Some people think they were beaten to it by 66 million years – by dinosaurs . . .

DID DINOSAURS BEAT US TO THE MOON?

An asteroid hit the Earth 66 million years ago and sent most of the dinosaurs to extinction. The force of the impact was so great that it shot huge chunks of Earth not only into the air, but out in to space, through a hole that had momentarily been created in our atmosphere. These chunks of Earth rock then solidified and melted into black glass-like objects, before falling back to Earth. We call these glassy objects tektites. (And it's thanks to tektites that we recently learnt that the dinosaurs went extinct in spring.)

It is thought that while a lot of the chunks of Earth that shot into space fell back to the Earth, much of it would have continued out into the universe, and embedded in those rocks would have been the bones and fossils of dinosaurs. Some geologists have even suggested that these bones may have made their way to the Moon, or even Mars!

Which means that one day, when we return to the Moon, we can test their theory out by going fossil hunting for dinosaurs.

THE FUTURE OF SPACE

There's one more thing I think all Impossible Investigators should look for in the sky. It's an incredible object, and it requires you to think far into the future. Because one day, roughly 8 million years from now, two small brass disco-ball objects are going to crash into Earth.

Orbiting roughly 3,700 miles above our heads are two satellites called LAGEOS-1 and LAGEOS-2 (Laser Geometric Environmental Observation Survey 1 and 2). These 24 inch spheres are passive (meaning they have no electronics inside them), but are simply covered in multiple retroreflectors (that give the impression of a very expensive golf ball). Their mission is to determine exactly how long a day on Earth is, what the shape of the Earth is, measure the planet's gravitational field and map the change in size and shape of the continents. To get this data, scientists simply beam a laser at each of the LAGEOS satellites each year and take measurements from the time the beam is sent and when the reflection returns it.

But that's not the only job for these disco balls in the sky. Attached to the satellites are some time-capsule-like plaques designed by astronomer Carl Sagan. These plaques are there to help humanity in the future understand why a couple of big brass disco balls have just crashed into Earth. The plaque shows how the continents look now on Earth, how they looked

268 million years ago and then finally a prediction of how they will look on the day they crash back on to Earth.

I wonder who will be here to see it. Will they be human? Would my 8-million-year-old descendants be looking out for it like I was that night in Bath?

It was midnight in Bath and I still couldn't see the planet discovered on this street – Uranus. I suddenly remembered there is an app for your phone that shows you exactly where in the sky all the stars and planets we've mapped are. It's great fun. You hold it up to the sky, move it around and it tells you everything you need to know. I started searching. Ah, it turned out I didn't come at a good time. The planet was currently on the other side of the world. In order to see it, I would have had to dig a hole through the centre of the Earth. Instead, I just stared at the ground in between my feet and imagined I could see it.

'Are you OK, mate?' said a passing man. 'What are you looking at?'

'I'm looking directly at Uranus,' I replied.

'OK, no need to be rude,' he said as he walked on.

I sniggered and headed home too.

CHAPTER 10
ARE WE ALL ACTUALLY LIVING IN IN A GIANT VIDEO GAME SIMULATION?

I am hugely excited because I have made a discovery that might just help to answer this question, one of the biggest mysteries of all time.

You see, there is a theory that this universe isn't actually real. That it's all just one big computer simulation and all the things in it are just bits of data, and that you – yes, you reading this book right now – are just an avatar, a character in the game, and when your time in the simulation is done, who knows what will happen. Maybe you'll find you're actually a nine-armed purple alien sitting in some weird intergalactic arcade, having just finished playing a popular new game called *My First Earth*.

Interestingly, scientists are really looking into this. Not the purple alien bit – I made that up. But many are convinced the computer simulation theory might be true. In fact, some think the chances of us living in a game, or a matrix, is as high as 50%! And right now there are tech billionaires who are funding scientists to try to break us out of the simulation.

So, how do we prove if this is true or not? We look for clues. Or, as they have come to be known, glitches.

A glitch is when the universe's coding gets its wrong.

There are many clues to look for. One of them is when something suddenly changes, but the universe somehow forgets to wipe the memories of those who remember when it was different. For example, there are people who are convinced that former South African leader Nelson Mandela died when he was imprisoned in the 1980s. He didn't. In fact, he got out of jail, served as president from 1994 to 1999 and would eventually die in 2013. It seems mad that anyone could think he had died in prison, but the weird thing is that many people have the same memory. Was that a glitch in the matrix?

These things are happening all over the place. Another one my friend Joel told me is about a children's book series called *The Berenstain Bears*.

'That's not how it's spelled,' insisted Joel.

'What do you mean?' I asked him.

'It's Berenstein. It's always been Berenstein, and now suddenly the universe has glitched and it has been changed to Berenstain. Someone's switched the "e" in "stein" for an "a".'

And Joel's not the only one who remembers it being Berenstein. Thousands online have shared their memories of it being different. And I must confess, I am one of them. I am convinced it was Berenstein when I was a kid.

There are millions of people out there right now, just like me, playing detective and trying to spot mistakes in the 'game'.

Coincidences are another type of clue to look out for.

Have you ever been told about, or experienced yourself, an amazing coincidence that is so great, so huge, that it has made you stop and think, *Hang on . . . something is going on!*

There's a word for it, too. Synchronicity describes coincidences that seem to be so perfectly timed and appear at such vital moments in your life that it's almost as if they are trying to tell you something. Like the universe is trying to guide you somewhere.

Well, I have found a coincidence so great, so impossible, that it has shot straight to number one on my list of **IMPOSSIBLE COINCIDENCES** in my **YOGIBOGEYBOOK** and should provide some solid support to help answer that big question:

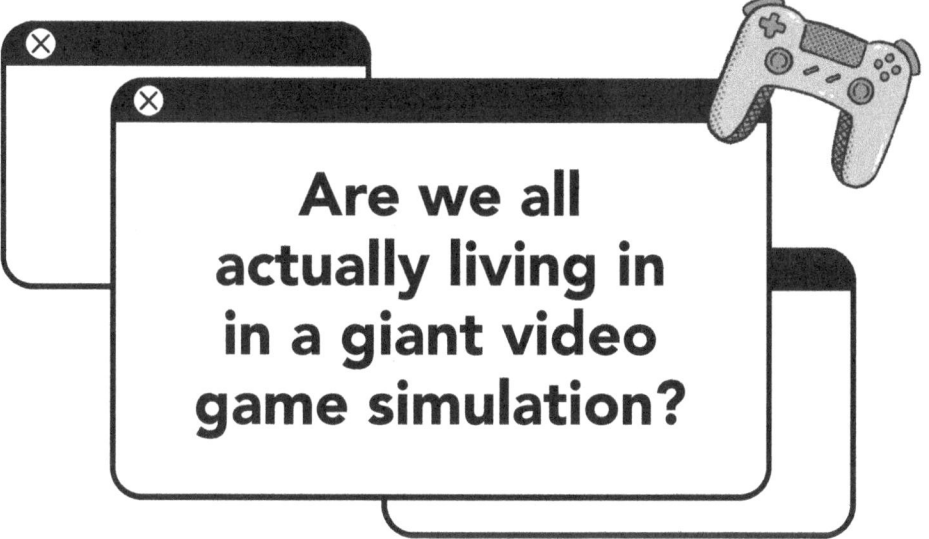

The discovery I made was this: the Roman Emperor Elagabalus invented the whoopee cushion.

Now, before I explain why this is such a huge discovery, I want to run through a list of all the evidence of coincidences that point to a video game universe in my **YOGIBOGEYBOOK**.

EXTRACT FROM THE YOGIBOGEYBOOK #6

THE BEST OF SYNCHRONICITIES

10. THE STORY OF UMBERTO AND UMBERTO

On 28 July 1900, the King of Italy, Umberto I, was out eating dinner in the town of Monza when the owner of the restaurant approached him. The King was confused: this man looked exactly like him. 'What is your name?' asked King Umberto.

'My name is Umberto,' the man replied.

How bizarre, thought the King. 'Where were you born?' he asked.

'In Turin,' replied the man.

'Double odd. So was I!' said the King. 'When were you born?'

'On 14 March 1844,' the man replied.

The King couldn't believe it. Triple odd! That was his birthday too! What was going on?

As they continued talking, the coincidences kept coming. It turned out that they had both got married on the exact same day, and each to a woman called Margherita. Their sons even had the same name: Vittorio.

'How long have you had this restaurant?' asked the King.

'I opened up shop on 9 January 1878,' said the restaurateur.

'But that's when I was inaugurated as king!' the King replied.

The King was clearly taken in by these extraordinary coincidences, and as the night ended, he invited his fellow Umberto to join him at an athletics competition the next day. But the restaurateur never arrived. He mysteriously died the morning of the competition, in an accident involving a gun. The King was disappointed, but not for long. Later that evening, the King himself was shot to death by an assassin.

9. THE CASE OF THE PLUM PUDDING

A similar strange set of coincidences once happened to a man named Emile Deschamps. Emile only ate plum pudding three times in his entire life. The first was when he was at school, as it was recommended to him by a man named Mr de Fontgibu. Ten years later, Emile ordered plum pudding at a restaurant, only to be told by the waiter that the last pudding had already been ordered, but the man who had ordered it was willing to share it with him. That man was Mr de Fontgibu. What a coincidence! Emile would tell this story to his friends when he was over for dinner some time later. They had just served plum pudding for dessert when Emile explained that this was only the third time he had eaten the dessert.

He was explaining the remarkable coincidence of Mr de Fontgibu when the doorbell rang. It was Mr de Fontgibu! He wasn't meant to be there. He was going to have dinner with a friend in another apartment in the same building, but had accidentally rung the doorbell to the wrong door!

8. WITH GREAT POWER

Ringing the doorbell to the wrong house is one thing, but it's nothing compared to the coincidence that took place at 20 Ingram Street, Queens, in 1984. Andrew Parker, his wife, Suzanne, and their two daughters were living at this address when letters, postcards and magazines all addressed to Peter Parker (AKA Spider-Man) started arriving in their post. They were followed by phone calls, all asking to speak to Peter Parker. Andrew thought he was being pranked by local kids who had worked out his surname. What he didn't realise was that, by extraordinary coincidence, in the *Spider-Man* comic books, the address for Peter Parker's home, Aunt May's house, is 20 Ingram St, Queens. The very same address as the real-life Parkers!

7. THE PRESIDENT WHO SAVED HIMSELF

In February 1981, the fortieth president of America was standing in Ford's Theatre in Washington DC when he suddenly found himself shuddering. This was the room where President Abraham Lincoln was famously assassinated. It made him think of the number of presidents who had been killed, and it occurred to him that the same fate could be waiting for him. His name was Ronald Reagan and he was a former Hollywood movie star turned president.

Nine days later, a man called John Hinckley Jr. fired six rounds at the President as he was walking out of a hotel. As soon as the gun was fired, Reagan's Secret Service team leapt into action. One of them, Jerry Parr, grabbed the President and threw him into the back seat of the waiting presidential limousine. As they sped off, heading for the White House, Parr immediately diverted the limo to the nearest hospital. It was against all protocol, but it was a decision that would save the President's life. Doctors said afterwards that had he arrived even just 5 minutes later, he would have died.

Parr became a hero, receiving numerous honours and medals; however, he believed it was fate that he was there that day.

You see, the only reason Jerry Parr had become a Secret Service agent was because as a kid his dad took him to the cinema to see a movie called *Code of the Secret Service*. He became obsessed with the film and watched it multiple times, deciding that he wanted to be a Secret Service agent when he grew up. The character he loved most was Brass Bancroft, who was played in the film by . . . Ronald Reagan.

'I didn't save you,' Parr later told the President. 'You saved yourself.'

6. ATTACK OF THE GIANT SQUID

In Jules Verne's adventure novel *Twenty Thousand Leagues Under the Sea*, the submarine captained by Captain Nemo is attacked by a giant squid. This scene became famous, but events like this virtually never happened in real life. In fact, one of the very few times we know that it definitely happened was when a giant squid was seen attacking a ship in 2003 – it was a vessel that was competing in the Jules Verne Trophy race.

5. THE IMPOSSIBLE GOODBYE NOTE

In the summer of 1913, a man was walking his dog along a river in Glanmire, Cork, in Ireland, when he spotted a bottle on the banks of the river. An actual message in a bottle. The message read: 'From *Titanic*. Goodbye all. Burke of Glanmire, Cork.' The note had been written by Jeremiah Burke, a nineteen-year-old farmhand who was travelling to America to visit his sisters. As he was boarding the ship, Jeremiah was handed a bottle containing holy water by his mother. According to this story, at some point on the journey, Jeremiah wrote his note, put it in the bottle, tied it with a bootlace and threw it overboard. Somehow, that note travelled halfway across the North Atlantic Ocean, all the way to the coast of Ireland, and ended its journey literally a few miles from Jeremiah's family home. The bottle was found by a man who knew Jeremiah. He walked it over to the home, where the family were shocked to confirm that it was his writing.

4. THE IMPOSSIBLE BATSMAN

Gaylord Perry was a baseball player for the San Francisco Giants. He was an incredible pitcher, but a terrible batsman. So terrible, in fact, that when journalist Harry Jupiter was watching a game, he heard the Giants' manager Alvin Dark say, 'There'll be a man on the Moon before he ever hits a home run.' Ten years later, on 21 July 1969 humankind did stand on the Moon. Back on Earth, and just one hour after Neil Armstrong and Buzz Aldrin landed on the lunar surface, in a game against the Los Angeles Dodgers, Gaylord Perry hit his first home run.

3. THE MAN WHO PREDICTED THE SINKING OF THE *TITANIC*

There once was a journalist called W.T. Stead, and he did a pretty extraordinary thing. He wrote a story that predicted a major disaster years before it happened: the sinking of the *Titanic*. The *Titanic* was a ship pitted to be 'unsinkable', but on its first voyage across the Atlantic it collided with an iceberg and sank, killing most people on board, as there were not enough life rafts to save everybody. In Stead's story, written years earlier, a ship travelling from Liverpool to New York collides with another vessel, which it doesn't see in the fog. Before this happens, the main character in the story wanders the deck and takes note that there are not enough life rafts on board to fit all the people on the ship. And this wasn't the only story Stead would publish that had an eerie connection to the *Titanic*. Stead wrote about another transatlantic sea tragedy with only a few survivors. The captain in the story was based on the captain of the RMS *Majestic*, Edward Smith, who would go on to captain the *Titanic* in real life. Sadly, Stead wouldn't write many more stories, because he died as a passenger on board the *Titanic*.

2. THE UNBELIEVABLE TALE OF TU YOUYOU

In at number 2 is the story of Tu Youyou, who made a life-saving discovery.

Tu Youyou is my favourite name of any scientist. Her first name, Youyou, is literally the sound a deer makes when it is bleating. It was picked by her father from a line in his favourite poem ('Deer bleat "youyou" while they're eating the wild qinghao').

In the 1960s, millions of people were suffering from malaria, so the Chinese government tasked Tu Youyou with the job of trying to cure it. Rather than do what everyone else in science was doing – using modern medicine to find the cure – Tu Youyou studied ancient Chinese remedy books. Incredibly, she found the cure. It was in a thousand-year-old book called *Emergency Remedies to Keep Up One's Sleeve*. Her discovery saved millions of lives, and she was awarded a Nobel Prize for her work.

The extraordinary bit of synchronicity in this story is the fact that, according to Tu Youyou, it appeared as if she had been destined to find the cure. You see, in the poem that Tu's father took her name from, the bleating deer is chewing on a single plant. And of all the thousands and thousands of different species that plant could have been, by incredible coincidence, it was the same plant Tu Youyou found to hold the cure for malaria! And not only that, when Western scientists began using her discovery, they gave it the name 'artemisinin' after the Greek goddess Artemis, who is always accompanied by just one animal – a deer!

1. THE INVENTOR OF THE WHOOPEE CUSHION WAS CALLED BASSIANUS!!!

So here we go. In at number 1 is my favourite discovery. The person credited with inventing the whoopee cushion is the Roman Emperor Elagabalus. Now, this doesn't sound very coincidental. That is until you learn that Elagabalus wasn't his real name. It was a name he took on when he was made emperor. His real name was Sextus Varius Avitus Bassianus. BASSI-ANUS.

THE INVENTOR OF THE WHOOPEE CUSHION WAS CALLED BASSIANUS?!

The universe is a simulation. No one can accidentally have a name like that and invent a whoopee cushion! There can't have been a copy-and-paste set of Umbertos walking the Earth at the same time! None of these things should have happened! But they did.

Now, why are the Bassianus and Tu Youyou stories occupying top positions on this list? It's because they are also showing us something that many scientists have been looking into, which is name-synchronicity. Or: another possible clue to a glitch in the matrix!

I myself am a victim of name-synchronicity. My name is Dan Schreiber – a pretty normal, boringish-sounding name. I used to get annoyed by it at school. I wanted a cool name, like my friend Max. His real name was Maximilian, but everyone used to call him MaxiBILLION. Now that's a name!

Fortunately, I later learned that I didn't have to change my name at all. It's weird enough as it is. You see, I'm a writer. That's what I do for a living. And the reason why that's weird is because my name is what I do. Schreiber translates from German as 'writer'. So that means my name is Dan Writer. Did I become a writer because of my name? That's impossible, surely. Well, as odd as it sounds, there are people out there studying this who are hoping to find out if a name does have an influence on what you do with your life. It's called nominative determinism, which means someone's job matches their name.

For example, the fastest man ever is called Usain Bolt. There's a weather presenter called Sara Blizzard. The current president of Nintendo America is called Bowser.

The most successful tennis player ever to take to the court is called Margaret Court. There's a defensive footballer called Mark De Man. Anna Smashnova was Israel's top tennis player. The one-time fastest female hurdler in the world was Marina Stepanova. And then there's diving champion Svetlana Filippova.

The first great collector of these names was a journalist called John Hoyland, after he spotted a book on the north and south poles by a writer called Mr Snowman, and a scientific paper on people who pee their pants by two scientists called J.W. Splatt and D. Weedon.

Everywhere you look there are countless examples of people who are perfectly named for their jobs. Could there be something to it? Even on the bookshelf in front of me, right now, I can see some. There's my book on coincidences written by a man called Dr Surprise.

And it's not just authors that have this – pick any job, like dentists! There's a dentist in America called Rachel B. Pullin, who be pulling teeth all day long, and there's another one there called Dr Toothman. Back in the UK there's a dentist in London called Doctor Fang, and out in the town of Oakham you can visit the Dentith & Dentith Dental Practice. There's actually a theory that you are more likely to become a dentist if your name is Dennis or Denise. I imagine the same must be true for brain surgery: how many Brians and Briannas are there working in that area? Actually, saying that, there is a magazine called *Brain*, which used to be run by a man called Dr Brain. And before him, it was headed up by a man called . . . Mr Head! There are so many examples in the medical world. One paper that tried to prove this point was written by four doctors called Limb, Limb, Limb and Limb.

Have you ever looked up what your name means? It may seem impossible, but sometimes a name can take you places in life. Even to the Moon. Just ask Buzz Aldrin, the second astronaut ever to walk there. His dad's surname was Aldrin, but do you know what his mother's was? Moon.

A BAD TIME TO BE CALLED CHASE

KEEP ON THE LOOKOUT

We have no idea what any of these coincidences mean. Is it the universe glitching? Possibly. Though we must all remember that in an infinite universe, impossible coincidences can and will happen. As the great Sir Terry Pratchett put it, one-in-a-million chances crop up nine times out of ten.

Still, the feeling you get when you notice a glitch for the first time is a truly wonderful thing. And I hope you experience it one day, whether you believe in it or not, because it can change the way you view everything and remind you to look around and marvel at this impossible universe, video game or not, that we find ourselves in. Actually, I think I just got that feeling. Did you get that feeling? I swear I just experienced a glitch. Look back to the question I asked at the start of this chapter. **Are we all actually living in a giant video game simulation?**

I swear an extra 'in' has suddenly appeared in the sentence that wasn't there before? Who knows. But it's definitely one to log in the **YOGIBOGEYBOOK**.

EPILOGUE
WHAT HAVE ZOMBIES EVER DONE FOR US?

So here we are, at the final few pages of our Od<u>dy</u>ssey, and I am sitting on an Underground train, heading into North London on one last quick night-time adventure. As I sit and reflect on everything that's been written in these chapters, I can't help but think of Ken. (Not the Barbie one. The one with a time traveller friend from chapter 4.)

Ken taught his daughter to never believe in anything. 'Now listen, Daisy', he would tell her. 'You mustn't believe in anything. Instead, you should *suppose* in things. Don't say "I *believe* flying saucers are real",' he told her, 'Say, "I *suppose* flying saucers could be real". Suppose in ghosts,' he said, 'suppose in fairies, even suppose that the universe is a video game. But listen to me, Daisy. Whatever you do, don't *believe* it.'

I want you to remember that incredibly important nugget of advice from Ken. Or better yet, jot it down in the front of your **YOGIBOGEYBOOK**. Because not everything you have read in this book should be taken as 100% absolute truth. That's why they are called **IMPOSSIBLE THINGS**. It is a fact that people believe the Loch Ness Monster exists, but it is not a fact that it does exist.

From ghost chickens to imaginary friends – everything you have read in this book sits in the file marked 'unbelievable' and comes from stories, encounters and claims. They are not all scientifically proven. Remember your lessons from the very beginning of this book about my friend Tom not needing to use toilet paper after going to the loo, and repeat after me: *Tom does not have a magical bottom.*

So why do we bother looking into it at all? Well, because it's incredibly important work. And one day, if we do discover that ghosts exist, or that aliens are landing on Earth, or that time travellers are visiting, then we can all hand over our **YOGIBOGEYBOOKS** to the scientists studying it and they can use our work as research to help understand it more. The **IMPOSSIBLE THINGS** are also helping the world now, in other ways you don't appreciate. Take zombies, for example.

Did you know that, according to students at the University of Leicester, if every zombie bit just one new person a day, it would only take a hundred days for them to turn everyone into one of them?

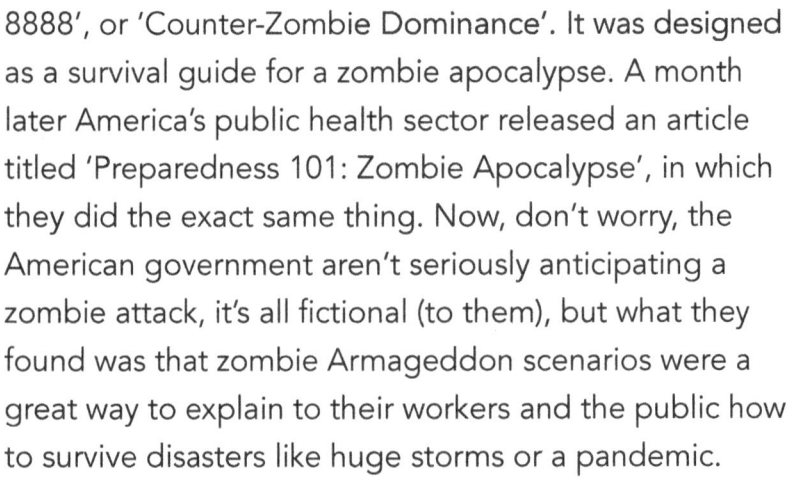

Fortunately, many people have taken measures to stop any oncoming zombie apocalypse – including the US government, who in 2011 put together a report called 'CONPLAN 8888', or 'Counter-Zombie Dominance'. It was designed as a survival guide for a zombie apocalypse. A month later America's public health sector released an article titled 'Preparedness 101: Zombie Apocalypse', in which they did the exact same thing. Now, don't worry, the American government aren't seriously anticipating a zombie attack, it's all fictional (to them), but what they found was that zombie Armageddon scenarios were a great way to explain to their workers and the public how to survive disasters like huge storms or a pandemic.

In fact, this very point was proven when a few years ago, in 2020, we were all locked in our houses trying to escape the COVID-19 global pandemic. Psychologists at Penn

State University worked out something interesting. Those who had watched lots of zombie and alien movies prior to the pandemic were better at dealing with what was happening, because these movies had prepared them for what could happen.

As John Johnson, the psychologist who carried out the research, put it, it was a rehearsal. These stories are not just entertainment, he said, they are preparation for life.

So what have monsters, ghosts, aliens, time travellers, telepaths, talking plants, imaginary friends, curses, alien satellites and guys called Umberto ever done for us?

They have helped us to cope and make sense of this impossible universe we find ourselves in.

Though seriously, just in case you are worried about the zombie thing, don't be. It's all fine. I was recently chatting to my friend Dr Erica McAlister about it.

'It can't happen. They'll never take over the world, and it's because of flies,' she said. Erica is the senior curator of Diptera and Siphonaptera (flies and fleas) at the Natural History Museum in London, and she has been thinking about this a lot recently.

The reason flies would thwart any zombie takeover is because zombies are dead, and therefore made up of rotting flesh. And flies love rotting flesh. So if suddenly there were zombies running around, it would be fine, because there would be a huge boom in the fly population and they would eat all the rotten flesh, cartilage and internal organs on the bodies of the zombies, and once that's gone there would be nothing to hold the zombie bones together.

So zombies could be real, but maybe we just don't know it yet because they are getting eaten before they get a chance to eat us.

Anyway, all this is going through my head as I arrive at my destination on the London Underground and make my way to the exit to complete the final mission of this book.

You see, I realise that the real purpose of an **IMPOSSIBLE INVESTIGATOR** is to tell these stories – to family, friends ... anyone! To champion them and make sure they're not forgotten, because you never know, one day they might change the world. Even if they are small things like reminding people to look out for that weird half-elephant, half-human lagoon monster called Narrie the next time they're in Sydney, Australia, or getting a Guinness World Records title for the world's oldest ghost – if enough of us do it, it will make a difference.

And that's why I've travelled to North London, because of a little-known story that I think needs some championing. It concerns the sixteenth- and seventeenth-century philosopher Francis Bacon.

Francis Bacon died because he was trying to prove an **IMPOSSIBLE THING**. He was riding home in a horse and carriage with his friend late one snowy night in North London, when he announced a theory. He had been thinking about how to keep food, like meat, from going off – see, they didn't have refrigerators in the 1600s.

'What if we froze the meat we eat, so that, rather than it going off after a night or two, you could keep it good for months?' he said.

'Nonsense,' replied his friend. 'It'll never work.'

'Yes, it will,' said Francis. He then became so determined to prove his friend wrong right there and then that he jumped out of the carriage, ran to a nearby house and knocked on the door. 'Do you have any chickens? I need one to prove a point,' Francis asked the confused old woman who answered the door.

As it happened, the old lady did have chickens and promptly killed and plucked one for him. Taking the chicken, Francis and his friend headed to a park around the corner, and Francis proceeded to bury the chicken in

the snow. He planned to return in a few days to dig it up and show that it was still edible. Unfortunately, Francis would never get to see the results of his experiment. You see, the cold that night had got to him: he immediately fell ill and died a few weeks later of pneumonia.

Francis Bacon is now said to haunt one of the local pubs in the area called the Gatehouse, where he sometimes accidentally scares the staff members as they're walking around the basement.

Some people might call Francis Bacon **'WEIRD'** for his experiment with the frozen chicken, but what he was trying to achieve wasn't impossible. If Francis had survived, he would have invented the freezer. Had he not died, he and his chicken would have changed the world.

Oh, and whatever happened to the chicken he buried back in the 1600s? Well, it haunts Pond Square in Highgate to this day.

And so we come full circle in our story. As I walk through the square, I look out for the chicken one last time, before heading into the Gatehouse pub. My mission today is to get recognition for Francis Bacon and the frozen chicken inside the pub, so that all kids visiting can learn about the story. As it stands, there is no recognition that either Francis or the ghost chicken exist. No plaque. No painting on the wall. Nothing. And I want to change that. Remember, it's the small things. And so I'm going to call over the manager and pitch my idea. All I'm asking for is a little nod to the legend. I'm going to request they add a new item to the their menu: a 'Chicken and Bacon sandwich'. It would mean that every time some kid ordered 'The Francis' (as I'm calling it), the waiter could then lean over and blow their mind with the tale of this truly **IMPOSSIBLE THING**.

Wish me luck, and until we meet again . . . stay weird.

Writing a book about impossible things was sometimes very nearly impossible. There were often differing accounts of stories, the facts usually changed with every retelling, and sometimes you'd find an absolutely brilliant story but when you went back to read it again, it had apparently glitched into thin air leaving no trace behind and making me look like a lone looney insisting it once existed.

Like those stories, this book would have glitched out of existence too if it wasn't for the hard work of my brilliant editor, Helen Archer, who is apparently capable of bending the rules of time (and the limits of human patience), because without that – as well as her wise advice and sharp editorial eye – this book would not be in your hands now. Thanks/sorry, Helen.

Huge thanks also go to Kristyna Baczynski, my brilliant illustrator, who perfectly captured the essence of the world of the impossible and sketched it on to the page, and to Jen Alliston, who did a stunning job of designing the book. I am so proud that thanks to her vision I now get to hold in my hands a book that looks exactly like the one I always wished I had as a child.

To the members of my SECRET WEIRDOS COMMITTEE, Micah Bell, Emma Govan and Mark Vent, this book would be poorer, factually questionable, and a whole lot less fun to write if it weren't for your tireless help and enthusiasm. I look forward to all the adventures to come.

Huge thanks also go to …

… the rest of the Wren and Rook team: Lara Hing, Victoria Walsh, Maz Brooks, Fi Evans, Namishka Karia, Karis Pearson, Katherine Fox, Laura Horsley, and Emily Lunn (who kicked the whole thing off) – thank you all so much.

… my powerhouse book agent Ben Dunn who makes my eyes light up with joy every time I see his name appear on my phone, as it means a new exciting book project is ahoy! (Also apologies to my everything-else-agent Nik Linnen who conversely goes a sickly green every time he sees Ben's name appear on my phone.) Big thanks to Theo Close too.

… to Joel Hill, Mitchell Brooks and Arron Harrison, my life long best friends, who had me believe that Tom Ellis had a magical bottom. Again, Tom, I am SO SORRY.

… to Rhys Darby, Leon 'Buttons' Kirkbeck, and everyone at my Cryptid Factor family, Rosie, Finn, Halina and Jarvis. For everything from the thunderbirds to the aliens of Giant Rock.

… to James, Anna, Andy, Alex, John, Sarah, Tara, Leying, Jack, Coco, Manu, and Ethan – AKA the Fishbusters. Ten more years! Ten more years!

… to my family, all the Schreibers, Bates, Rezks, Peaches, Smiths, Joynts, Engelhardts, Mosses and Gardners. If your weirdo story didn't make it into this book, don't worry, you haven't escaped just yet, it'll be in the next thing.

… to Spooky Al Riddell and Chris Lander at Global for allowing me to log the impossible things people of the world think every week.

… to the next generation, Sofia, Aless, Lola, Ayla, Sebastian, Felix, Iris, Celeste, Atlas, Theo, Raffi, Martha, Isaac and Kit. I hope this book makes you think weirder.

To my late grandmother Marguerite. Flat out the most brilliantly impossible person I've ever known.

And to the main players of this book (and my universe) Fenella, Wilf, Ted and Kit: I love you.

Lastly, to the most important person of all, without whom none of this could have happened, my biggest thanks must go to the wonderful Arnold Bottomleeeeeewhhhaaaaat???!!! NO, get out of here, Arnold Bottomley! Gah. Always ruining the ending of a book.

DAN SCHREIBER

Dan Schreiber is an award-winning author, podcaster, comedian and investigator of all things impossible. He is the host of the hit no.1 podcast *We Can Be Weirdos*, and is co-host of two others: one about monsters called *The Cryptid Factor*, and another about interesting facts called *No Such Thing As A Fish*. He also co-created the long-running BBC Radio 4 series *The Museum of Curiosity*.

Dan was made and assembled in Hong Kong, learnt to be weird at school in Australia and now lives in the UK with his wife and three kids. He goes nowhere without his **YOGIBOGEYBOOK**.

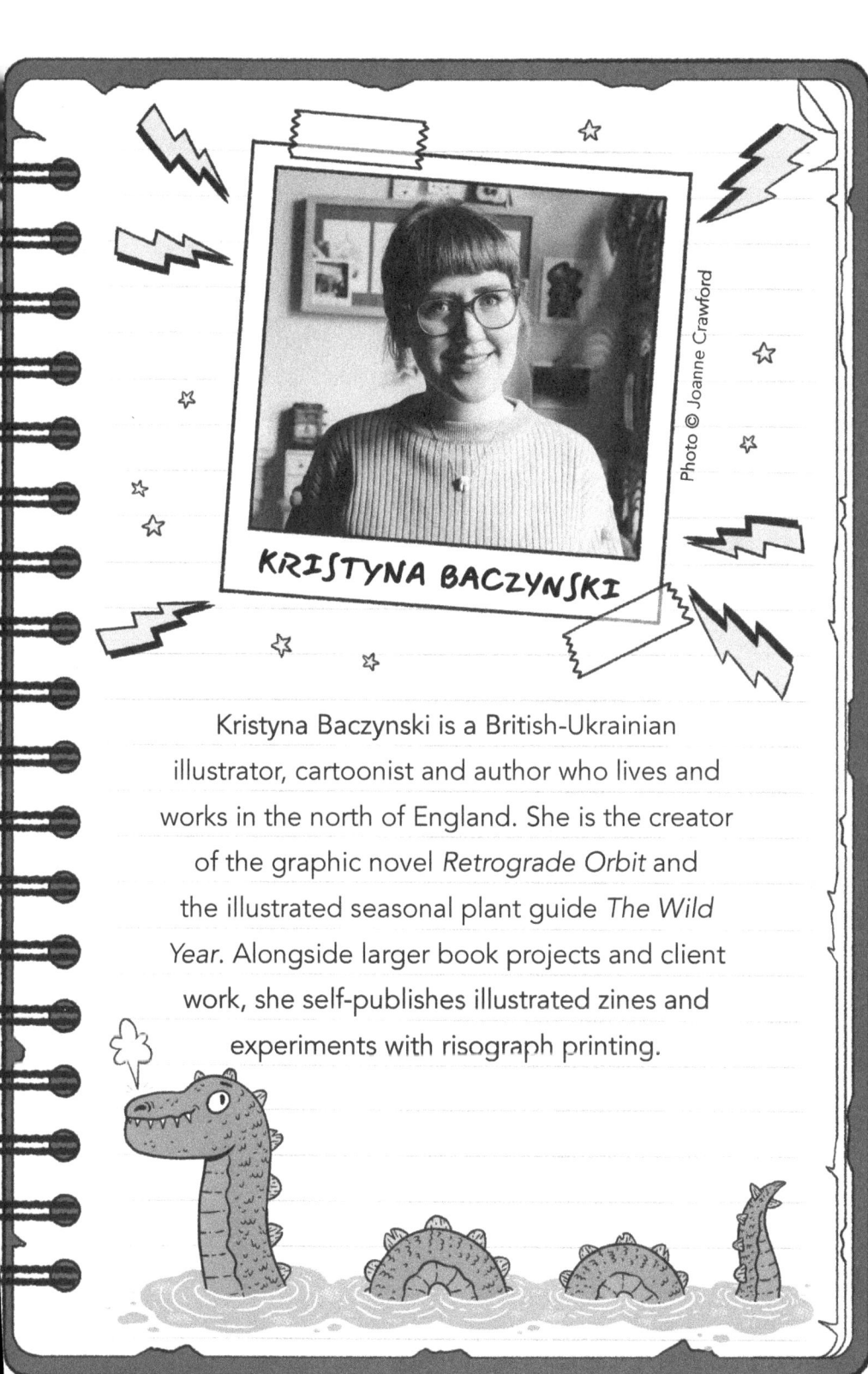

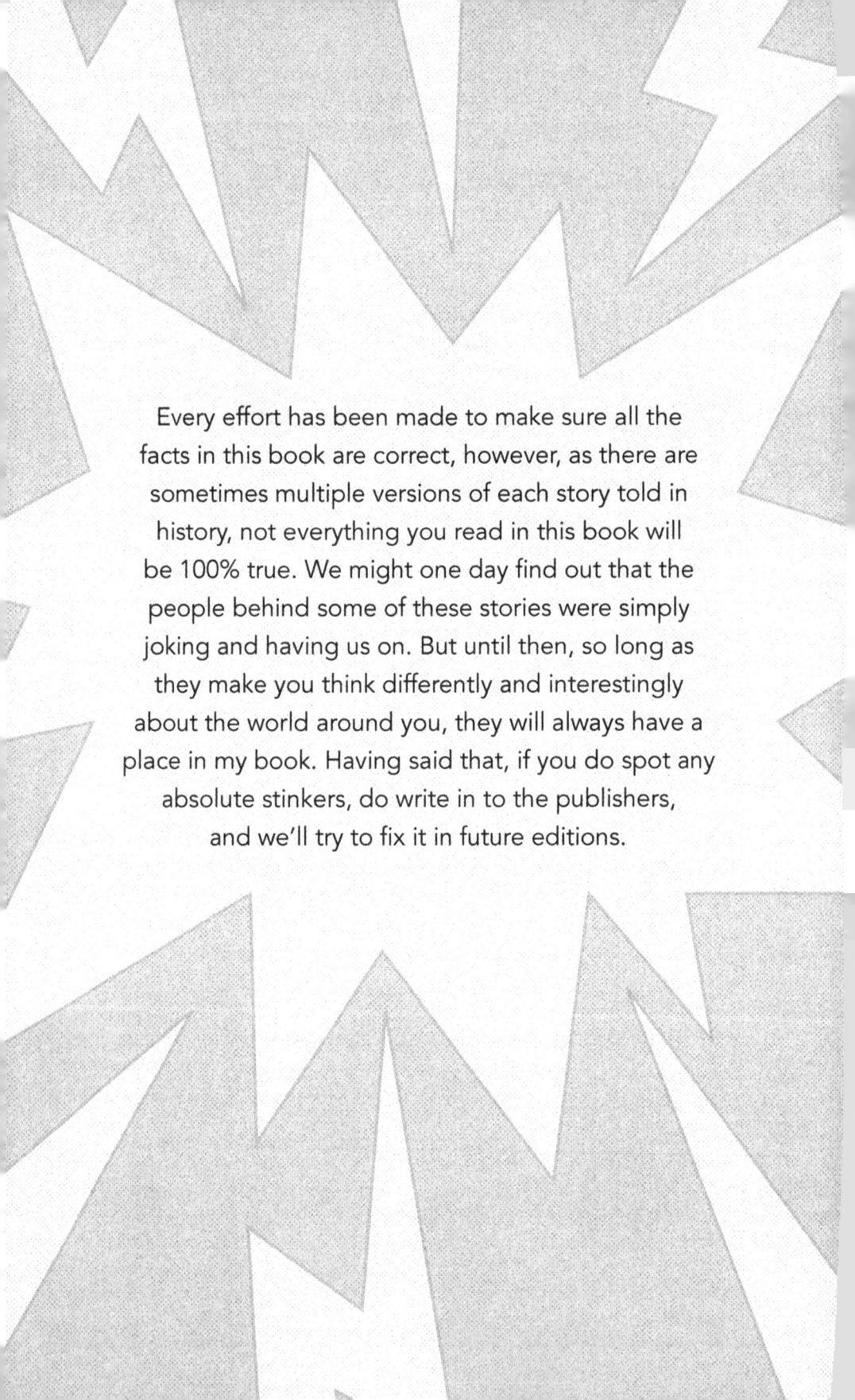

Every effort has been made to make sure all the facts in this book are correct, however, as there are sometimes multiple versions of each story told in history, not everything you read in this book will be 100% true. We might one day find out that the people behind some of these stories were simply joking and having us on. But until then, so long as they make you think differently and interestingly about the world around you, they will always have a place in my book. Having said that, if you do spot any absolute stinkers, do write in to the publishers, and we'll try to fix it in future editions.

If you liked this book, why not try ...